ARAB SCIENCE:

Discoveries and Contributions

ARAB SCIENCE

Discoveries and Contributions

by EDWIN P. HOYT

THOMAS NELSON INC., PUBLISHERS

Nashville   New York

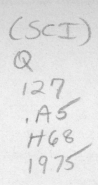
Copyright © 1975 by Edwin P. Hoyt

All rights reserved under International and Pan-American Conventions. Published in Nashville, Tennessee, by Thomas Nelson Inc., Publishers, and simultaneously in Canada by Thomas A. Nelson & Sons (Canada) Limited. Manufactured in the United States of America.

First Edition

Library of Congress Cataloging in Publication Data
Hoyt, Edwin Palmer.
  Arab science.
  Bibliography: p.
  Includes index.
  SUMMARY: Describes the development of scientific knowledge in the Arab world and its influence on the West during the Middle Ages.
  1. Science—History—Arab countries—[1. Science—History—Arab countries] I. Title.
Q127.A5H68   509'.17'4927   75-4597
ISBN 0-8407-6442-1

Contents

ARAB SCIENCE:

Discoveries and Contributions

1

The Coming of
the Arabs

ARAB SCIENCE and culture arrived just in time. In the seventh century, when the new religion of Islam stung Arab peoples into a ferment of growth and expansion, the West was stagnating. The Christian world lay in the throes of the Age of Faith. Earthly learning was despised and neglected. The teachings of ancient authors fell into disuse, and their writings were sometimes deliberately destroyed as "pagan." Wars raged among the Romans and Byzantines and the wild robber tribes of the North. Cities were sacked, and great libraries went up in flames. Another century of warring and wasting, and perhaps all the learning of Greece and Egypt would have been lost.

But Arab civilization had respect for knowledge. At the last moment, it stepped in and saved what it could of the work of the past.

The word "Arab" is derived from an ancient Semitic word which means "desert." The Arabs themselves call their peninsula *Jazirat al-'Arab,* which means "Island of the Arabs." They are an old people, and in spite of the ebbs and flows of civilizations across the Fertile Crescent, the Arabs were left fairly well alone because of the loneliness of their nomadic way of life and the harshness of much of their land.

Parts of Arabia were conquered, in varying degrees, by the kings of the ancient world, but they were seldom held for long. At the height of Roman power, Augustus Caesar sent the prefect Aelius Gallus out from Egypt with ten thousand men to conquer Arabia. The Romans marched through the burning heat of day and camped in the freezing cold of the desert night. They fought a few engagements here and there, but day after day the army withered away in this unfriendly land. In a few months the Romans turned about, made their way to the Red Sea, and were ferried across to the more friendly lands of Egypt.

Western students of the ancient world knew very little about the Arabian desert and the way of life of its people. Herodotus was told wild tales about the fertility of the land. He was impressed by the frankincense and myrrh, the cassia, cinnamon, and laudanum that came from the desert, but he did not understand that some of these were desert products and some came by trade from as far off as India. The Roman Strabo knew of the unfriendly nature of the land. Pliny in A.D. 70 spoke of temples and palaces, of beautiful cities that he had never seen. These men were most impressed by the products they secured from the people of Arabia. As for the correct knowledge of the land, by far the best description was that of Ptolemy the Alexandrian, who collated reports from travelers in this far part of the world between A.D. 150 and 160 and drew the first "scientific" map of the Arabian peninsula, one based on actual observations.

The Sabaeans of southwest Arabia, who developed the first-known Arab civilization long before the birth of Christ, were navigators and traders, and they knew the uses of astronomy in finding their position by the stars. They had a written language (sometimes called Himyarite) with twenty-nine characters in its alphabet, a language derived from the ancient Egyptians. These were the people of the Bible's Sheba, and their general area was that which is now known as Yemen. The level of Sabaean technology was very high compared with that of the rest of the world. They built a great temple at the capital city of Sirwah, whose ruins later housed a village of a hundred people. East of Sanaa they built a new capital called Marib and provided water for it by building a great dam.

This capital was moved about 115 B.C. to Zafar, near the modern town of Yarim, about four hundred miles southeast of Mecca, by the new Himyarite dynasty. These rulers lived in palaces and castles, not tents. Greatest of these was the castle of Ghumdah in Sanaa, which was built of granite, porphyry, and marble, with a roof of marble so transparent that it was said the king could look out from his court in the top story and distinguish between kinds of birds flying above. These Himyarite kings made coins of gold, silver, and copper. They also worked in bronze, which meant they had learned to combine ores. But with invasion of the East by Alexander and the coming of the Greek Ptolemies to control Egypt, sailors from Greek Egypt and later Roman Egypt learned to move through the Red Sea into the Indian Ocean. As the sea power and trade monopoly of the Himayrites was lost, their civilization declined and stagnated. By the middle of the sixth century A.D., the Himyarites had been conquered by the Abyssinians from Africa, who built a grand Christian cathedral on the site of ancient Marib.

The Arabic language comes from the Nabataeans, who lived to the north (originally in what is now Jordan). They made their capital at Petra on an arid plateau 3,000 feet above sea level. For several hundred years, until the beginning of the Christian era, Petra was a key point on the trade routes leading east from the Mediterranean. The Nabataeans spoke Arabic, but they wrote at first in Aramaic, which was the language of the intellectuals, just as Latin was the cultural language of Europe for many years. But by the third century A.D. the Nabataeans were writing in the script that would become the Arabic of the Koran, and since Petra was such an important trading place, this writing spread through northern Arabia.

In the last thousand years of the pre-Christian era, various other civilizations grew up in Syria and along the northeast section of Arabia. Principal among these was that of the Lakhmid dynasty, which had its capital at al-Hirah, not far from ancient Babylon, west of the Euphrates. These kings and their people also wrote in Aramaic and spoke Arabic, and al-Hirah transmitted its knowledge of this written language to the Quraish, the rulers of the city of Mecca, who would soon become the leaders of a whole new world movement.

This was the real beginning of Arab science, when writing and culture came to a strong tribe. Here is the situation of Arab culture in the sixth century after the birth of Christ:

The Arabs of the deserts were virtually untouched by the learning of the philosophers and scientists in Asia and in Europe. Their calendar was the calendar of the moon, and they did not worry about the difference between the 354 days of that calendar and the 365 + days of the actual year. (The modern year is adjusted every four years by adding the "leap-year" day, February 29.) Rains and droughts were brought by the will of the various gods. The Arabs worshiped some three hundred gods, who had their homes in the Kaaba, the sacred temple in the middle of Mecca. They believed, for example, that the rain was caused by the new moon which sucked the water from the sea, far to the west of their lands, then sent the rains to them at the will of the gods. They knew the stars and constellations, and used them to guide themselves on the desert at night, but they had no rational theory of cosmology, nor did they concern themselves about the physical composition of the universe.

Their medicine was folk medicine. They knew the uses of many herbs and other substances, from practical experience. They circumcised their sons for cleanliness. But they also believed that strong odors brought disease and that jinns, or earthly spirits, controlled much of their lives. They treated smallpox with red clay diluted in water, pouring it in the sick one's eyes. For various pains they burned the skin of the area involved. Some Arabs were versed in the art of setting broken bones. Others treated various diseases and wounds skillfully. But no scientific literature existed as such, nor was there any philosophical questioning of the sort that leads to scientific discovery.

In this society, at the turn of the seventh century, there lived a young trader and caravan leader named Muhammad. He was of the ruling class of the Quraish tribe that lived in Mecca, his grandfather having been the leader of the military forces and guardian of the sacred well Zam-

Zam and the Kaaba. Muhammad was a perfectly ordinary
man, it seemed. He married at the age of twenty-five and
was lucky enough to find a rich wife, Khadijah, whose
wealth brought him a certain amount of leisure. In the
year 610, Muhammad "received the call" to go out and
preach the tenets of a new faith, the belief in a single
god—Allah.

His preaching began peaceably enough. He was
friendly to the Christians and the Jews, holding that they
had strayed from the paths of the true faith, and inviting
them to return under his guidance to the ways of the
one God. But as months and years went on and he was
spurned by Christians, Jews, and his own idol-worship-
ing fellow citizens, the religion of Islam took on a more
warlike and punitive note. In 622 Muhammad migrated,
with his followers, from unbelieving Mecca, where the
Muslims had been persecuted, to Medina, where he was
assured of the support of two Arab tribes. For the next
eight years Muhammad and his followers fought for sur-
vival. The ranks of the Muslim movement were swelled
by converts from among the slaves of Arabia (whom
Muhammad freed if they embraced Islam) and the nomadic Bedouin, who appreciated his warlike leadership.
Many battles were fought, from skirmishes to full-scale
war, and some were lost while others were won. But the
strong spirit of Muhammad and the belief in the one God
spread swiftly among the desert men of Arabia, and in
630 Muhammad conquered Mecca without a struggle,
tore the idols from the Kaaba, and consecrated that holy
place to the service of Islam.

Control of the Holy City extended the influence of
Muhammad and of Islam to every corner of the Middle

East. Muhammad lived only two years more, but when he died in A.D. 632 his new religion was firmly established in Mecca and Medina, and his followers were eager to set out to conquer all Arabia and beyond in the name of the new faith.

They picked up the wand of civilization just as it was falling from the hands of the decaying Roman Empire.

What the Arabs Conquered

MUHAMMAD'S death was to have a far-reaching influence on the development of Arab and Muslim society—and thus on Arab and Western science. When Muhammad was alive, he was the spiritual and political leader of the Arabs. But all his children except his daughter Fatima died before Muhammad, and he did not designate a successor. One possibility was his cousin, Ali, an early follower and a trusted general, who was Fatima's husband. But Ali had antagonized Muhammad's favorite wife, Aisha, and she schemed to keep him out of the caliphate, the leadership of Islam.

Thus, from the beginning, Islam was split into factions, the most important of which were to be the Hashimite, named for Hashim, Muhammad's great-grandfather, and the Umayyad, named for Umayya, Muhammad's great-uncle.

Abu Bakr, the first caliph, was Muhammad's father-in-law and did not belong to either faction. But he was an old man and could not be expected to stand in the way of ambition for long.

Abu Bakr's caliphate was marked by revolution in the desert, where the tribes felt that, when Muhammad died, so did their responsibility to pay taxes to Medina. Under the vigorous but bloodthirsty general Khalid ibn-al-Walid, the Muslims crushed and united the Arabian peninsula. Having done so, they then moved outward against the crumbling Byzantine Empire to the north and west and the equally weakening Persian empire to the east.

The Arabs were turning, thus, toward two great civilizations, which had long histories of scientific and cultural accomplishment. To the north, despite wars, there still remained a vast compendium of scientific knowledge amassed by Western societies, ranging from the technology of the Egyptians, through the science of Chaldea, to the natural philosophers of Greece (Thales, Anaximander, Anaximenes), including works of mathematicians, astronomers, physicians, geographers, botanists, and physicists. To pass on this accumulated knowledge, the Ptolemies had established the Museum in Alexandria —a kind of university, with lecture halls, dormitories, and dining rooms. It was divided into four disciplines, literature, mathematics, astronomy, and medicine. Connected with the museum was a great library, the largest in the Western world, which contained 400,000 volumes. But before the coming of the Arabs, this institution had begun to fail. In the year A.D. 390 the Bishop Theophilos destroyed the Serapeium Library, which held the overflow of books from the great library, because he regarded its pagan books as anti-Christian.

On the other side of Arabia, Persian science and the Persian culture dated back to the seventh century B.C. and the times of Zoroaster, the philosopher and prophet. The Persians built canals and founded schools of medicine. Particularly with the coming of the Nestorian missionaries to Persia, much knowledge of Greek science was brought to the region, for the Nestorians translated scientific and medical works into Syriac and Persian. Some time around the fifth century A.D. the Persians established a school at Jundishapur, near Kazerun, which by the sixth century was the great intellectual center of its time. Here came together the ideas of East and West, the science of the Greeks, the technology of the Romans, the philosophies of the Jews and the Syrians, and the science of Hindus and Chinese. Here were made Persian translations of Aristotle and Plato. The philosopher Paul the Persian wrote commentaries on the works of Aristotle. Others here wrote history and translated works from the Sanskrit of the Indus Valley.

In 634 the Persians gave in to the army of Arab General Khalid ibn-al-Walid, and the way into Persia was opened. Then came the march on Syria. In both areas, the Arab tribesmen quickly showed how ignorant they were. They traded gold for silver because they had never seen silver before. They gave away fortunes because they could not conceive of sums above 1,000 (ten hundred).

But as these Arabs moved onward through Persia, they learned. They captured the eastern shore of the Persian Gulf and occupied Persepolis. On the banks of the Euphrates the Arab General ibn-abi Waqqas showed how fast he had learned. He built a magnificent palace modeled on the royal palace of Persia. The reed and mud huts of the common Arab soldiers gave way to brick houses, and the Arabs built a new city at al-Basrah on the edge of the Tigris estuary. It was to become an intellectual center of Arab life in the eastern wing of their empire.

Meanwhile, another Arab army was moving west under

'Amr ibn-al 'As, another of the faithful generals from the days of the Prophet. In 640 the fierce 'Amr led 4,000 riders into Egypt until they were outside the gates of the present Cairo. There they waited for 6,000 reinforcements, and then the fortress was besieged by men who knew nothing about sieges. But again they learned quickly. At the end of seven months the Arabs had learned to fill the moat, scale the walls, and overpower the garrison inside. The Arabs then moved down the Nile Delta, taking one town after another along the river, until the army, now 20,000 men, stood before the walls of Alexandria, capital of Byzantine Egypt. Ahead of them, above the walls of the city stood the museum and the library, and the soldiers looking up could see the two slender obelisks erected by Thutmose III, the temple to Caesar begun by Cleopatra, the palaces of the rich, and the tower of Pharos, the lighthouse on the spit. Suddenly the Arabs were in possession of the intellectual jewel of the Mediterranean.

While the Arab troops were marching, the rulers in Medina were beginning to feel the need for a more ordered existence, so in 633 Caliph Abu Bakr put the scribe Abu Saad Zaid ibn-Thabit ibn-al-Dabbak al-Ansari to work collating, transcribing, and assembling the suras, or verses, of the Koran as handed down by Muhammad. One might say then that Zaid ibn-Thabit, in his attempt to put the Holy Law in order, represented the very earliest intellectual study of the Arabs. The revision became the absolute authority of Islam and the Arabic language, and has never been changed since.

The second caliph, Omar, was an intensely religious

man who adhered to the antimaterialistic views of Muhammad. When Muhammad died, his possessions consisted of a suit of armor, a cloak, a palm mattress, and
the bare necessities of life, and Omar once appeared in
Jerusalem in such ragged clothes that the Greek patriarch
was contemptuous of this conqueror. When Amr sent an
emissary from Alexandria to Medina to announce to
Omar that he had captured 4,000 villas with 4,000 baths,
40,000 Jews to pay the poll tax, and 400 places of entertainment for the wealthy, Omar congratulated the emissary and then invited him to share his meal—his usual
simple fare of bread and dates and water. Omar also
used to walk the streets carrying a whip, with which he
struck down drunkards and others who broke the Holy
Laws. His caliphate was brought to an end in 644 when a
discontented slave became furious against a judgment
handed down by the caliph over a debt, and stabbed
Omar to death as he came to the mosque to say his
prayers.

Before he died, Omar appointed a council of Islam's
elder statesmen to choose the new caliph. They chose
Othman, the son-in-law of Muhammad, who had once
faithfully led the Muslims into Abyssinia in the early days
of persecution at Mecca. Othman was a member of the
Umayyad branch of the Quraish family, and he began
bringing Umayyads to high office. General Amr was
brought back from Egypt, and Othman's foster brother
Abdullah succeeded him. General Saad was recalled
from Iraq, and Othman's half brother al-Walid ibn-
Uqbah succeeded him.

Under Omar, the Arabs had been forbidden to own
property outside the Arabian peninsula. The idea was to

keep the Arabs separate and dependent on the caliphate in Medina, which would dispense all wealth and privilege. The people outside the fold, all non-Arabs, would live in peace, but they would never be first-class citizens.

But with Othman things changed quickly. His relatives learned of the wealth of Persia, and the Umayyads began migrating in that direction, given grand estates by their kinsman the caliph. Here the Arabs were exposed to marvels such as they had never before seen. At Ctesiphon, Damascus, Jerusalem, and Alexandria they encountered the fruits of ancient civilizations. They saw the art works of the ancient Persians and began to copy them. They found the columned temples of the Romans, and they were awed. They were exposed to the jewels and manufactures of Jerusalem. Their curiosity was aroused by the intellectual attainments of the thinkers of Alexandria, seat of Greek scientific culture such a short time before.

Among the learned men at Alexandria was the Jewish physician Aaron, who wrote a medical encyclopedia in the Greek language at about this time, an important work covering much of the medical knowledge of the then Mediterranean world. The Arabs came, they saw, and they wanted this material. So the encyclopedia was translated into Syriac and Arabic—and became the first Arab encyclopedia. But this tide of conquest sometimes flowed roughly, too.

After the original capture of Alexandria, all went well for several years, but in Constantinople the Byzantines regretted giving up this star of the imperial crown without a struggle, and they schemed to retake Alexandria. Caliph Othman's foster brother Abdullah, the ruler of

Alexandria, grew coarse and careless in the new luxury,
and the Arab garrison was reduced to a thousand men.
The Byzantines sent an army and a fleet of three hundred ships to attack the city, and slaughtered the garrison.
Even Othman could not countenance Abdullah's weak-
ness, so General Amr was sent back to recapture Alexandria, which he proceeded to do in 646, and such was
his rage at the Byzantine duplicity that he turned the city
over to the soldiers for sacking. The library of Alexandria was then destroyed, and Aaron's encyclopedia
was lost in the confusion. Both the Greek and Syriac
versions of Aaron's encyclopedia were lost, and all that
now remains is a part of the Arabic translation long
enough for historians to try to reconstruct what once was.

When Aaron was working in Alexandria, so was another encyclopedist. He was Paul of Aegina, a Greek
who wrote several works, including books on gynecology
and toxicology (which have been lost) and a seven-
volume encyclopedia of Mediterranean medicine, which
was saved from the sacking for later translation into
Arabic.

Another influential Greek thinker of this period was
John of Alexandria, a bishop who was also called John
the Grammarian. John was very popular with the Arabs
because he disavowed the belief of the Christian Church
in the Trinity of God. (The greatest point of difference
between Christianity and Islam, as Muhammad saw it,
was the stubborn refusal of the Christians to accept the
one God, indivisible.)

John the Grammarian became a favorite of Amr's and
was allowed the freedom of the city. He wrote on the
works of the ancients, Galen and Hippocrates, books that

dealt with medical arts, fevers, the pulse, anatomy, and the causes of disease. The Arabs who came to Alexandria saw the wonders of these books, they spoke to the learned men, and they realized that a new world of knowledge was unfolding before their eyes. The world owes much to unknown and unsung Arabs. All that is known, for example, about the translator of Aaron's encyclopedia into Arabic is that he was named Masarjawai.

The Syriac language became the link between the Arabs and the languages of the people they conquered. Syriac became a tongue of learning, and quite early much of Greek thought was translated into it. Sergios of Theodosiopolis, for example, translated many treatises on agriculture and several works of Galen and Aristotle into Syriac before he died in Constantinople in A.D. 536.

In the seventh century, then, the Arabs were moving all through the area we know as the Middle East. They were established in Egypt, Syria, Iraq, and Persia, or Iran. The degree of culture was very high, for the Syrian Christians carried Greek culture with them as they migrated east. One such was Severos Seboht of Nisibis, who translated part of Aristotle into Syriac. He was a philosopher, scientist, and a bishop, head of the monastery of Qen Neshre on the Upper Euphrates. This monastery was the major center of Greek learning in the area, and there students learned geographical and astronomical subjects. There, too, they carried out practical studies of eclipses and used the plane astrolabe, which they built from a Greek model.

The astrolabe, one of the first successful scientific instruments, consisted of a suspended disk, whose edge was marked with the degrees of a circle. By moving a

pointer fixed to the center, an observer could determine
the relative positions of the stars. The astrolabe was a
basic instrument of navigation too.

Thus Severos Seboht's work was practical as well as
intellectual. He also discovered the nine Hindu numerals.
(These are the "Arabic numerals," which are in common
use today.) A distinguished man thinking far beyond his
time, he was the first to declare that science could never
be the monopoly of any nation, but belonged to the
people of all nations.

Another important early figure in Arab learning was
George, bishop of the Monophysitic Arab tribes of Meso-
potamia, who lived in al-Kufah where the Arabs established their early center.

The Monophysites were offshoots of the Christian
Church, who broke with Christians over the divinity of
Jesus Christ. What is important to Arab history is the
fact that they were Arabs and spoke the Arabic language.
So as the Arabs moved east and west and north under
their first caliphs, they carried along their contributions to
science—and something else, that language. If Jew or
Copt, Christian or Zoroastrian in Egypt or Syria were to
understand his captors, he must learn their Arab tongue.

At first the Arab conquerors did not particularly encourage non-Arabs to become Muslims, but soon the ad-
vantages of Muslim life in a Muslim society began to ap-
peal to the conquered. To become a Muslim one must
learn Arabic to read the Koran, for it was forbidden to
translate this Holy Book. Thus began in the area of Arab
sovereignty.

It was not all easy. The spread of the language and
of the civilization was slowed considerably in 656, when

Othman's rule aroused so much rebellion among the foes of the Umayyad part of the Quraish tribe that eventually Othman was assassinated. The new caliph, Ali, was the first cousin to Muhammad and, since he had married the Prophet's favorite daughter Fatima, his son-in-law. Muhammad's widow, was still alive, and she hated Ali. She had gone to live at al-Basrah near the Persian Gulf. There she joined other dissidents in a military campaign against Ali. The dissidents lost, Aisha was captured, and she was sent gently back to Medina, where Ali could keep an eye on her.

The capture of Aisha did not end the revolution, however. More fighting went on, which ended in a stalemate. Ali and Aisha's general, Muawiyah the Umayyad, agreed to an arbitration of differences. Ali was deposed and ultimately murdered, and Muawiyah was put in his place. In 661 Muawiyah established the first hereditary caliphate, that of the Umayyads, and made a big change. He moved the capital of the Arab world to Damascus.

The stress and strain of this period prevented the Arabs from giving much thought to scholarly pursuits, but just before Ali was deposed, he had suggested that the scholar Abu-l-Aswasal-Duali make a study of Arabic grammar. Thus, Abu has come down to us as the first Arabic grammarian, and Ali as one of the earliest devotees of science and learning for their own sake.

After Ali's murder the Alist empire was divided into two parts. Muawiyah was in control of the western half, and the followers of Ali were in control of the eastern. Within a few months Muawiyah had gained the allegiance of the followers of Ali, and the march of Islam could begin once again. Yet the march was not really headed,

and differences between the followers of Ali and Muawiyah continued to erupt.

Yet, for the next eighty-nine years the headquarters of
the caliphate would be at Damascus. All the empire was
divided into five viceroyalties, whose realms indicated
the scope of empire. Iraq, Syria, and eastern Arabia were
under one governor. Hejaz, Yemen, and southern Arabia
were under another, Armenia and the area between the
Tigris and Euphrates another. Egypt and North Africa
were one province, as were western and eastern Persia.
One can see, then, that the Arab empire extended far—
from the border of India to the Strait of Gibraltar. It was
then the most potent force in the world.

The center of power of the Arab world changed. The
power had been held in the heart of the Arab peninsula.
It would be so no longer.

5

Umayyad Culture

THE UMAYYADS created in Arabia the conditions under which it was possible for learning and science to prosper. Muawiyah was an enlightened man, and he loved comfort and pomp. The first attribute taught him that he must modernize his government and take it out of the hands of the *irnams* or priests. The second attribute caused him to praise and encourage learning as signs of luxury and for amusement, and during his reign there would be twenty years of peace and much prosperity.

Even during the civil war Muawiyah and his successors had taken steps to build a strong government in Damascus. Muawiyah established an office of records and a postal service. He also established a climate in which non-Arab converts to Islam could rise high in government service and gain great wealth. Here, one might say, was a vital clue to the cultural and scientific development of Islam. Muawiyah's personal physician was a Christian whose name became ibn-Uthal when he converted. He rose to become financial administrator of a province. A Greek named Sergius who had helped secure the Arab victory in Damascus was rewarded with a high office, and his grandson became the playmate of the future Caliph Yazid. So the Umayyads were gaining a tolerance for

foreigners unknown before their time and a respect for
what those foreigners might have to offer.

By the beginning of the eighth century, then, the
centers of culture of Islam were Damascus, Alexandria,
al-Kufah, and al-Basrah, although these latter places were
infiltrated with discontented men who called themselves
Shiites.

In the early days at Damascus, Caliph Muawiyah
created gardens and great public works, and Amr ibn-al-
As, the conqueror of Egypt, ruled over the cultural center
of Alexandria with wisdom and serenity, too.

The Umayyads set out to create a grand new culture.
They built great mosques and other public buildings.
Their palaces were marvels of cool white stone and shin-
ing fountains. With the coming of peace, there was also
time for princes to indulge in intellectual pursuits, and of
course royalty had to set the course because only the very
rich could afford the luxury of learning for its own sake.
In the eighth century one of the leading lights of civilization and science was Muawiyah's grandson, Khalid ibn-
Yazid ibn-Muawiyah, an Umayyad prince. Khalid was
deeply interested in medicine, astrology, and alchemy.
He encouraged the translation of Greek scientific works
into Arabic, and this alone would have been adequate
reason for such a powerful prince to be styled "the
philosopher," as he was.

Under the peaceful conditions of life at Alexandria,
the Greek philosophers certainly could continue their
work. The political ferment in the eastern regions, however, was something else. Muawiyah had appointed al-
Mughirah ibn-Shuvah as governor of al-Basrah, and when
Mughirah died, Yazid became ruler of Arabia, Iraq, and

Persia, ruling through a secret service of 4,000 men. The main purpose of these 4,000 was to unmask the Shiites, the followers of Ali, and bring them to justice, which in this case meant death. So while peace seemed to reign in Damascus, the western half of the empire was soon bathed in blood.

In 683, Yazid's son, Muawiyah I, succeeded but proved totally inadequate to rule and quickly abdicated, so the Umayyad council then turned to another branch of the family. Soon the caliph was Abd al-Malik, who faced the continuation of rebellion in the southern and eastern parts of his realm. Still, in spite of all his troubles, Abd al-Malik built the great new mosque, the Dome of the Rock, in Jerusalem, to divert many pilgrims from going to the troublesome territories. He sent generals off to subdue the Shiites, and then he turned to science and art of government.

Abd al-Malik's predecessors had found Greek, Syrian, and Persian administrators in their new territories, and had been so busy with their conquests that they had given much responsibility to these foreigners. Abd al-Malik decided that the Arabs must learn to govern their empire, and he set about teaching them, planning that in two generations the Arabs would be capable of administration. He also invented the Arab coinage, replacing the Roman and Persian coinage with the first Arab coins: a silver dirhem, which was worth a dime, and a gold dinar, worth about a dollar.

To settle the internal problems of the eastern regions once and for all, he sent as governor to al-Kufah a former schoolteacher named Hajjaj ibn-Yusuf, who became the most bloody governor in Arab history. Arriving in al-

Kufah, he rode his horse to the mosque, tore off his turban, and turned to the crowd that had assembled to hear him.

"O people of Kufah," he said, in his most melodramatic way, "I saw before me heads ripe for the harvest and the reaper, and verily I am the man to do it . . ." He was indeed. Hajjaj was viceroy of Iraq and Persia for twenty-two years, and in that time he put to death 120,000 people. On his death 80,000 more were in prison. All the empire shuddered when his name was mentioned. And yet he brought a kind of tremulous order to the land. After the eastern part of the region was molded as he wished, he then turned north and east. For the next decade Arab troops were marching in Afghanistan, Turkestan, and Uzbekistan (the latter is today part of the Soviet Union). This army of 50,000 men took Bukhara and Samarkand and reached the borders of China. Another army took the land of the Indus, moved to Hyderabad, and then into Baluchistan and the Punjab, coming up against the culture of the Buddhists of the East.

By 716, when Hajjaj died of cancer, the empire had spread far to the east, and Persia and Iraq were completely under control. Cultural centers were established at Bukhara and Samarkand. Abd al-Malik had decreed that Arabic should be the official language of the empire, and so the culture began to be handed down in Arabic.

From Damascus, the Umayyads had headed north to butt up against the Turkish civilization. They went west, beyond the borders of Egypt, and conquered the lands of the Berbers in North Africa (Carthage was taken in 698) and moved as far as Tangier.

In 705 Walid succeeded. He introduced the minaret, the tall tower from which the faithful are called to prayer in the mosque. He was also the first ruler since the Romans to build insane asylums and hospitals for the chronically ill. Like his father he was a great builder and enlarged the mosque at Mecca, rebuilt the one at Medina, and converted the Cathedral of St. John the Baptist at Damascus into a magnificent Muslim house of worship.

Under Walid's reign the Umayyads moved even further in conquest. Musa ibn-Nosair, governor of the western territories and son of a Christian, consolidated the gains at Tangier. He chose a Berber leader, Tariq ibn-Ziyad, to be governor. That rise of foreigners is indicative of the speed with which the Arabs were assimilating the people they conquered.

The Berbers were sailors, and so in 711 it was no great adventure for them to cross the Strait of Gibraltar with a force of 7,000 men. In a few months the Arabs and Berbers had captured Algeciras, Malaga, Cordova, and Granada. A year later Musa came up into Spain with another army of 10,000 men, moved on to Salamanca, Valencia, Tarragona, and Barcelona. By the fall of 713 the Arabs and Berbers had taken nearly all of Spain.

Musa was recalled to Damascus in 715. When he marched triumphantly into the city, he brought with him four hundred captive Visigoth nobles, followed by 30,000 Spanish girls and many thousands more slaves and prisoners of war, carrying tons of gold and silver and jewels for the coffers of Islam.

Musa's triumph was short-lived, for Walid died. Suleiman became caliph, and he stripped General Musa of

wealth and power, murdered or brought back the other
powerful governors from their provinces, and comported
himself as what he was—the weakling tyrant of the
Umayyads. Suleiman was annoyed because the new conquests had been made by neo-Muslims. The Arabs were
members of the first social class, and they received pen-
sions from the government, according to their rank.
Below them were the neo-Muslims who were theoreti-
cally equal to the Arabs. In fact, however, neo-Muslims
depended entirely on the will of the official under whose
eye they fell. The third class was that of the "tolerated
sects," which included Christians and Jews. These people
were given a good deal of latitude. (For example,
Muslim law did not apply to them unless they were involved in a dispute with a Muslim. Otherwise their law-
giving was done by their own leaders.) At the bottom of
the social heap were the slaves, and in the eighth century slave trading was a brisk business all over Islam.
Slaves came from everywhere, by conquest and trade.
Among them the fair Spanish slaves brought the highest
prices, but the wide range of colors and nationalities
had a tendency to make of Islam a very democratic
society in a racial sense.

The conglomerate nature of the society was also a
contributing factor in the growth of knowledge. In spite
of Suleiman's objections, by the middle of the Umayyad
period, the empire was hardly "Arab" at all, for its
people consisted of Muslims of many nations.

In the days of the Umayyads the wealthy turned to the
cities of Mecca, Medina, and Taif in Hejaz on the Arab
peninsula. These became the pleasure centers of the empire, the homes of music and poetry and high life. Mean-

while, the eastern centers of al-Basrah with 300,000 people and smaller al-Kufah became the centers of the intellectual ferment. The central city of Damascus was the capital of political life. Alexandria declined in importance. The center of culture had shifted east in two centuries, and virtually nothing remained of the activity that had made Alexandria the scientific beehive of the past.

The primary study at these eastern Arab centers was the Arabic language itself. This study brought the comparison studies, philology and lexicography. Soon, the Muslims were also writing history and biography, largely so the state treasurers could determine just how much pension each Arab Muslim deserved from the public treasury. For every Arab got some money—just how much depended on the prestige of his ancestors. As the law of Islam was tightly bound to the Koran, the study of law also meant the study of literature and religion and naturally to philosophies. For example, the doctrine of *qadar,* or free will, was espoused by at least two of the caliphs. But the conservatives said there could be no relationship between Allah and such human ideas as power, wisdom or life—because Allah was above such human concepts.

Education was developing, for rulers and public— separate and unequal. The Umayyads sent their young princes to royal settlements in the Syrian desert, usually under the direction of some learned person. He might be an Arab or he might be a foreign Muslim, or even a Christian. At the court schools, the young men were taught the pure Arabic of the Koran. They learned poetry and the arts of desert warfare and hunting. They

learned to swim—a very important art to the Arabs after
they moved to the shores of the Mediterranean. They
learned the manly arts of the Bedouin: courage, hospi-
tality, and endurance. The common people might have a
Koranic education, too, but only by going to the special
mosques where classes were held. A handful were trained
as physicians, most of them relatives of doctors. The
Arabs held with succession, and a father would be succeeded by his son in practice.

The court physicians and doctors to the nobility of
the Umayyad dynasty came either from the Persian
schools or from the Greek medical schools. In either
case it was largely Greek medicine, brought to combine
with Persian medicine. Caliph Muawiya's physician was
ibn-Uthal "the Christian," and Majjaj's doctor was
Tayadhuq, "the Greek." Here, too, we encounter
Masarjawai, the translator of Aaron's lost medical encyclopedia. That book was the earliest scientific work
translated into Arabic.

In a sense the old scientific center of Alexandria was
moved bodily to the eastern part of the Arab empire.
The schools of medicine were transferred by the Caliph
Omar II between 717 and 720 to Antioch and Harran.
One might even say that Greek was no longer the language of science, Arabic was taking its place. That was
the biggest change of the eighth century.

The gradual betterment of the lives of non-Arabs
continued. Caliph Omar II consolidated the empire by
relieving neo-Muslims of special taxes. But he also
brought Arabs into administrative posts, and here many
of these warriors proved corrupt and incapable. That
was his ruin. The Umayyad caliphate declined. The

caliphs spent their time hunting or drinking or in the harem, where they listened to music and poetry rather than to the Koran and messengers bringing bad news from afar. The rulers revived the rigid class structure, made all but Arabs second-class citizens. Hardly had Arabia eaten the fruit of freedom, it seemed, before it was snatched away.

The result was quick disaster. In the caliphate of Hisham, whose rule began in 724, the Umayyads were in trouble again. The Greeks of the Byzantine Empire sensed the decadence of Damascus, and attacked Syria. Central Asians rebelled and so did the Berbers of North Africa.

In the west, in Spain, the Arabs and loyal Berbers had continued to advance the spread of empire until now. In 732 Governor Abd al-Rahman ibn-Abdullah led his troops across the Pyrenees and set his sights on Paris and Rome. But in the region between Tours and Poitiers, on a day of snow and ice, which the Arabs and Berbers detested, the Frankish Europeans rallied and fought back. They were in forest, where the Franks knew a kind of warfare quite foreign to the Arabs, and they were led by Charles Martel, grandfather of Charlemagne. Abd al-Rahman was killed in the battle, and his army retreated with its loot. This battle in 732 represented the high tide of the Arab surge into Europe. They would never cross the Pyrenees again.

The Umayyads declined, because they fell into almost total corruption. Wine drinking and gambling were absolutely forbidden by the Koran, but Caliph Walid II bathed every day in a pool of wine and spent most of his day drunk. The Koran demanded that women be chaste

and wear the veil, but the lady Sayyida Sukayna of
Medina was married eight times, took hundreds of
lovers, and told all husbands that she would do exactly
as she pleased. The lady Ayasha, a namesake of the
wife of the prophet, declared publicly: "Under no circumstances will I veil myself. God hath put upon me
the stamp of beauty and it is my wish that the public
should view that beauty. . . ."

The corruption of the cities was accompanied by another change. The Umayyads relegated the conquered
people of Iraq and Persia to second-class citizenship.
Since these descendants of an ancient culture were far
more learned than the Arabs, they chafed.

Then came the final political mistake. In 744 Yazid
III decreed that the old Arab belief in predestination
(God controls man's every action, giving him no choices)
be replaced by the rationalist doctrine of free will.
Logically this change should have stimulated the flow
of ideas. But with the Umayyads it became simply an
excuse for personal corruption. This rotten dynasty was
waiting and ready to fall.

It was too bad. Caliph Hisham was an able ruler, but
the excesses of his forebears had created a situation of
almost unceasing rebellion in every part of the Arab
empire. From Damascus Hisham could not concentrate
on troubles everywhere.

Hisham died in 743. The next year Yazid III became
caliph, the first product of the old liberal policy of mixed
blood. Yazid was the son of Caliph al-Walid and a female
slave who had been a Persian princess. So were Yazid's
successors of mixed blood. Ibrahim and Marwan II were
the sons of foreign women and Arab princes. Perhaps

that was the trouble. At least in the southern regions, the old followers of Ali allied themselves with descendants of al-Abbas ibn-al-Mottaleb ibn-Hashim—one of Prophet Muhammad's uncles. This group picked up support from the religious leaders who believed the Umayyads were perverting Koranic law and the old traditions. The rebellion began in Khurasan in northern Persia in 747 under the black banner that had symbolized Muhammad himself. Two years later the insurgents took al-Kufah, and on October 30, 749, they declared abu-Abbas, descendant of the Hashim family, the new caliph.

4

The Glory of
Baghdad

AS THE white banner of the Umayyads fell in April 750, Damascus surrendered. The Umayyad caliph, Marwan II, was tracked down and killed outside a mosque in Egypt, and the Abbasids then set about exterminating the Umayyads.

On June 25, 750, the Abbasid general Abdullah invited eighty Umayyad nobles to a banquet near Jaffa, and in the course of dinner he had them all assassinated. The hunt was on then until none were left but the youthful Abd al-Rahman ibn-Muawiyah. The Abbasids now ruled the Muslim world, and the new caliph built his capital on the left bank of the Euphrates River in the northern part of Iraq, because he did not want his city contaminated with the memories of the struggles of the past. Four years after his assumption of the caliphate, al-Abbas died of smallpox, and his brother succeeded to the caliphate. He took the title al-Mansur, under which he would rule for twenty-one years. For seven years al-Mansur occupied the palace of al-Hashimiyah that his brother had built, on the river between al-Dufah and al-Hirah, but then he laid the outline of a new city that was to be more splendid than anything in the world. He chose a place on the west bank of the Tigris. It would be known to history as Baghdad.

The city was built in four years by a hundred thousand
architects, masons, carpenters, artisans, and slaves
brought from all parts of the empire. It was a round city,
surrounded by double brick walls and a deep moat. Inside was a third wall ninety feet high with four gates, and
from them projected four great highways that extended
to the ends of the empire. In the center of the city stood
the caliph's palace, whose audience chamber beneath a
green dome rose 130 feet in the air. Most of the city
was built of stone taken from the nearby ruins of the
ancient Persian capital of Ctesiphon, itself once one of
the marvels of the world.

Al-Mansur discarded the old Arab ways and modeled
his government on the Persian. His court adopted Persian ways, and al-Mansur symbolized it all by first putting on the tall Persian peaked hat. Two solid Arab
traditions remained, however. Islam was the state religion, and Arabic was the state language.

In all else, the Abbasid caliphs gave themselves up to
Persian life and the enjoyment of luxury. The society
quickly became Persianized. The common dress was no
longer the cloak and headcloth of the Bedouin. The men
wore wide trousers, shirts, vests, and jackets. The women
wore dome-shaped caps, long dresses, and silver and
gold anklets, and they dyed the tips of their fingers with
henna.

The nobility no longer sat on the ground or on pal-
lets as the Arabs had. They sat on *diwans,* sofas that
extended around three sides of the room, or on cushions
on the carpets that covered the floor. They ate rich spicy
foods and cooled themselves with ice brought from the
mountains. In fact, an Arab writer quoted a formula to

"solidify water even in June or July," but the formula is long lost. The Arabs of the desert had bathed seldom and sometimes washed themselves with sand, but now the caliph built public baths and supplied them with hot and cold running water. The nobility took up new interests, including the highly intellectual game of chess. The Arabs encountered much that was new and different, and they examined each item with a bright and curious eye. Much earlier, the Arab conquerors had captured paper in Samarkand (whence it had come from China), and before the dawn of the ninth century Baghdad would have its own paper mill. And under al-Mansur the revival of agriculture began, with more attention paid to the canal network, once the backbone of the Tigris–Euphrates civilization, which had been allowed to disintegrate. A relative of al-Mansur's supervised the rebuilding of a great canal that connected the Euphrates at al-Anbar with the Tigris at Baghdad.

In this society, the leading places were occupied by the caliph and his family, the officials of his government, the various members of the Hashimite section of the Quraish, the children of Hashim, the tribe of Muhammad himself. These Hashimites were now courtiers and hangers-on, the officer class, and the higher civil service. But just below this rank was an upper class which consisted of writers, artists, doctors, men of the law and the Koran, and skilled craftsmen. In the needs of this new society in its new capital, it was easier for a man of brilliance and education to forge ahead than in any society since Ptolemaic Egypt.

The building of Baghdad opened the golden age of Arab science. It is symbolic that the plan of the city was laid out by al-Naubakht and Mashallah, astrologers to al-Mansur who were also mathematicians, engineers, and astronomers. Al-Naubakht was a Persian, Mashallah an Egyptian Jew, who represented the other end of the empire.

During the last years of the caliphate of al-Mansur, an Indian traveler came to Baghdad from the East, bringing with him the Indian Siddhantas, treatises on theoretical astronomy. The five Siddhantas were written by Hindu scientists in India, but they showed much evidence of the Ptolemaic thought. One of the Siddhantas was the foundation stone of Hindu trigonometry. One calculated the length of the year in the manner developed by Ptolemy of Alexandria, the geographer, who had taught as early as the second century A.D. that the earth was round.

When Caliph al-Mansur heard of the existence of the Siddhantas, he called in his astronomers, Ibrahim al-Fazari, his son Muhammad ibn-Ibrahim al-Fazari, and Yaqub ibn-Tariq. They met with the Indian traveler to learn of these marvels, and Muhammad was selected to translate the Siddhanta from the Sanskrit into Arabic, because he was the finest Arabic scholar who also knew Sanskrit.

The difficulty of this undertaking was enormous. Not having a mathematical or astronomical tradition, the language of Arabic had to be adjusted to accept the new concepts, words had to be coined and the terms explained.

But it was done, and again the Arab world was exposed to the Hindu numerals. This time the Siddhanta brought the numerals to the attention of the greater body of Arabic intellectuals.

This new information stimulated the astronomers of

al-Mansur. One of their difficult practical tasks had been to fix the point of the Kaaba, the Holy Temple, in Mecca, in relation to various points of the empire, so the faithful might turn to Mecca to pray. Now, Muhammad's father, Ibrahim, was the first to construct astrolabes. He also wrote a book on the calendar and on the uses of astrolabes and the uses of the armillary sphere in studying the stars.

An armillary sphere is a skeleton sphere, composed of rings, designed to represent the important parts of the celestial sphere. It turned on its polar axis within a meridian and a horizon. It was accompanied by a set of tables which showed the user the usual positions of the heavenly bodies.

So here began the Muslim scientific tradition of dividing the circle into ninety-six parts, as Archimedes had done long before.

At about this same time Mashallah, the astrologer-astronomer, was undertaking the study of the heavenly bodies and the uses of scientific instruments.

The intellectual ferment of Baghdad had begun.

5

The Translators

BEFORE there could be much progress in scientific discovery in the Muslim world, there must first be some way to bring together the knowledge of the past. Luckily, the caliph and his court were aware of the existence of a large body of scientific knowledge in India and Constantinople, where the fruit of Greek knowledge remained, and al-Mansur was in communication with the Byzantine court from time to time. He asked for Greek works of science, and the Byzantines sent him Euclid's works. Since Euclid was the great systematizer of the mathematical knowledge of Alexandria (his *Thirteen Books of Elements* remain the basis for the modern teaching of elementary geometry) the Muslims could not have been off to a better start.

But there were problems. One of the earliest translators from the Greek was Abu Yahya al-Batriq, who translated most of Galen and Hippocrates. Thus the Arabs learned what the ancients knew of epilepsy, diet, environment, and prognosis of disease. He did well with these. But when he tackled Ptolemy and Euclid and tried to work out mathematical as well as rhetorical problems, he ran into trouble. He had to take a Greek manuscript and translate it into Syriac, and from that translate the Syriac into Arabic. Why? Because in these early days of Arab power, few Arabs spoke Greek, although many spoke Syriac, and most of the foreign scholars who were fluent in Greek were not yet expert in Arabic.

Al-Mansur was a patient man. He listened to Abu's troubles and only asked for better translations. Abu kept his head and his honors.

Al-Mansur suffered from indigestion, and that is why medicine grew quickly in his reign. He heard a Nestorian doctor named Jirjis ibn-Kibril ibn-Bakhtyashu could cure indigestion. Presto. Jirjis was ordered to Baghdad. He took two students with him. After they had quieted the caliph's stomach, there was a lot of free time, and al-Mansur put them to work translating medical works from Greek and Latin.

While Jirjis and the other translators were struggling, the philologists or language experts were working to make their lot easier. Chief among these at the time was Khalil ibn-Ahmad, who lived in al-Basrah. Khalil was an Arab, born at Oman in southeast Arabia. He systematized Arabic grammar and compiled the first Arab word list or lexicon. Khalil died before this last was finished, and it was completed by one of his students, Sibawaihi, a Persian who worked at Baghdad and al-Basrah. Sibawaihi wrote an Arabic grammer which is still considered to be the definitive work.

Al-Mansur spent much money bringing men from the intellectual communities everywhere to Baghdad. Oddly enough, the greatest scientific figure of the period— Jabir ibn-Haiyon—was working without any official recognition in al-Kufah. But al-Kufah was a hotbed of rebellious Shiites, and al-Mansur was fighting the Shiites.

He did away with Muhammad and Ibrahim, the last of the descendants of Ali, for their preposterous claim to be true heirs to the throne—slaying Ibrahim just outside al-Kufah. Consequently, little is known of Jabir, whose name was Europeanized as Geber.

Jabir is regarded by historians as the leading scientific figure of the second half of the eighth century. Much of what he studied was nonsense—like making gold out of air. Still he did much original research in chemistry, and he was the first here to study the geological formation of metals, the making of steel, dyes, varnishes, and acids. Obviously if he had done nothing more than improve steel, he had done a great deal. As an alchemist, Jabir believed that lead could be turned into gold, if only men could discover the mysterious *al-iksir*. He never found it, but his writings led such later alchemists as Roger Bacon to continue the hunt for this "elixir of life" and thus inadvertently to develop the science of chemistry.

Like most alchemists Jabir worked secretly and mostly in the dead of night. No one even knew where his laboratory was. Then, two centuries after Jabir's death, when al-Kufah authorities were rebuilding the street near his home, they discovered his laboratory deep under ground. In it was found a mortar and a large piece of gold. What a revelation! Had Jabir found al-iksir after all? This discovery stimulated other Arab alchemists, and the search for an easy way to wealth was encouraged all over again.

But if there was no "secret" of gold to discover, as there was not, Jabir did discover much else. Long after the end of the Arab era, twenty-two of Jabir's works survived in Arabic. This is all the more remarkable because in modern times few books outlive their authors. Later, hundreds of other works were attributed to this mysterious character. Geber was the best-known alchemist until the time of Paracelsus hundreds of years later. His contributions to science were very real. He discovered calcination, the process of reducing a substance to a powder, usually by the application of heat, which is vital to modern chemistry. He also discovered evaporation, crystallization, and other processes. He achieved in the eighth century a height that was not surpassed by his successors until the fifteenth century.

In modern times, scholars are of two minds about Geber. It is suspected that later writers used his name and that much attributed to him is not his at all.

Geber aside, this period of Arab scientific history is notable for the gathering of the forces, the strengthening of the Arab language so it could accept new ideas, and the assembling of the old knowledge from the translations of Greek books.

The translators were lucky that Arabic was already a very expressive language with many fine shades of meaning. The lexicographers and translators worked together. The former established an inventory of the Arabic language, while the scientists made an "inventory" of Greek and Indian knowledge. Thus early translators put into Arabic the terms in Greek where they knew the Arabic equivalents. The remainder they left in Greek for later translators and lexicographers to refine.

Medicine came first. There already existed the school of Greek and Persian medicine at Jundishapur. Because of the movement of ibn-Bakhtyashu to Baghdad, the great Jundishapur medical school would soon move there too. When al-Mansur secured the works of Euclid and

Ptolemy and they were finally translated properly, the Arabs had a sound grounding in everything that was known anywhere of mathematics, astronomy, and geography. And to cap this came translations of the works of Plato and Aristotle, which gave intellectual stimulation to further discovery.

Al-Mansur changed the nature of the Arab world. For example, he no longer drew his personal guard from the ranks of the Arabs, but from the Khurasan and Turkoman tribes of the eastern part of the empire, and the Persians, now first-class citizens, reveled in new glory. Al-Mansur governed through a council of state, this council led by a *vizer,* who was responsible only to the caliph. The first vizier, Khalil ibn-Barmak, influenced the caliph to undertake the study not only of Greek but also Persian arts and sciences. When al-Mansur set out for Mecca on pilgrimage in 775, all was secure. So well had he governed that the year when he died there was scarcely a ripple in the empire.

At al-Mansur's death, the general cultural level of the Arab empire had grown immeasurably. The Arabs were now a civilized people. The greatest influence on the Arab was that of the *mawali,* or new Muslims, of Persia and Iraq, who were as glorified by the Abbasids as they had been downtrodden by the Umayyads. Also there was a joy of living and a new strength of spirit. No feat had seemed too great for the caliph and his followers. A hundred thousand men had built the planned city of Baghdad in four years, and now it was a center of international trade and scholarship, it had all the power of the Middle East, and was unrivaled as a world center except by Constantinople.

With this change came "Persianization." The Arabs

adopted Persian titles and married Persian wives. Persians moved freely through the new capital. They brought
the idea of delegated authority. The vizier, under the
Persians, had more power than any man but the caliph
himself. The vizier administered the treasury, collected
taxes, and appointed governors. In modern times we
call it the staff system. Al-Mansur had adopted the idea
to save himself work, and it worked all right for him,
but it, again, proved to be a weakening force, and a
few caliphs later would cause the decline of the society
that had grown so rapidly.

One of the astounding lessons of the history of the
Arab empire is that, almost as a dynasty took power, it
sprouted the seeds of its own destruction. So it happened
to the Umayyads almost as they entered Damascus to
build their capital. Now, in 775, only twenty-five years
after the fall of the Umayyads at Damascus, the forces
were at work to destroy the new Abbasids at Baghdad.

One basic schism developed in the matter of philosophy or way of life. Many Muslims moved toward the
liberal views that in the Western world would lead to the
growth of modern science, yet there were others in Islam,
even in the eighth century, who held a severe theistic
view. During the next three hundred years the rational
—or what the Greeks and Arabs called the peripatetic
—view of life would hold sway. The caliph searched for
all knowledge for its own sake. But the theists held that
the literal words of the Koran must be obeyed, and if
philosophy or science conflicted with the Koran, the
philosophy or science must be put down. In the end the
theists, who had lost most of the battles, would win the
war, and the science of the Arabs would wither.

But such change seemed far away in 775. There was

much to be done, and much joy and profit in the doing of it for the eager students of the Arab world. Dozens, scores, hundreds of books with totally new ideas came to Baghdad. The caliph provided the money and the leisure to exploit this knowledge.

Al-Mahdi succeeded al-Mansur as caliph, and he was as liberal as his father had been. The progress of science in his caliphate continued, and the scientific leader was Thiyufil ibn-Thuma, a Maronite who came from the western part of the empire. Thiyufil came to Baghdad with a great reputation as an astronomer and astrologer, and indeed became al-Mahdi's chief astrologer. Thiyufil undertook translation of the works of Galen, the Greek physician, and of Homer. The caliph consulted him before taking military action, before marriage, before doing anything important. The astrologer had tremendous influence on the ruler. And then Thiyufil undertook an original work, a chronology of the history of the world, which was a matter of immense interest. It was the first work of its kind, the first world history.

Al-Mahdi ruled only ten years, and his son al-Hadi ruled but one. Then in 786 there came to the throne the fifth caliph, al-Mahdi's second son, Harun al-Rashid.

Harun was as canny a ruler as his grandfather had been. Old al-Mansur's executioner had occupied a place beside the royal throne, on a leather carpet laid out on the floor to save the tile from the blood of those unfortunates who displeased the caliph. Now with the sword in one hand Harun led his empire. But Harun was even smarter than his grandfather. Under him Baghdad became the world center of wealth, beauty, and learning, and particularly of the new flowering of Arab culture, which was marked above all by its sciences.

6

Islam and Science

WHEN Harun al-Rashid was twenty years old, he led an expedition against Byzantium and penetrated as far as the Bosphorus, where he was bought off by a treaty that promised annual tributes, including "book for translation." Thereafter Harun sent raiding parties among the Greeks with the instructions to bring back books. When the young Abd al-Rahman of the Umayyads succeeded in escaping to Spain and setting up his own dynasty there, Harun had the good sense to make only one unsuccessful foray against Abd and then to let Spain go rather than weaken the empire by maintaining a costly, long-range war. A succession of American Presidents could have learned a lot from Harun al-Rashid.

Harun sought friendly relations with Charlemagne, king of the Franks, who in this ninth century represented the greatest power in Europe. Charlemagne was then consolidating medieval Europe into the Holy Roman Empire.

What a difference in civilizations!

Charlemagne's nobles gnawed their meat from bones, threw the bones to the dogs lying beneath the tables of their drafty unheated castles, and wiped their hands and blew their noses on their filthy robes. They worked little and bathed less. They knew virtually nothing of the glory that had been Greece and Rome. Their idea of "public works" was a defensive wall built around a city. They had no ideas at all of "public health." Their understanding of medicine, the universe, natural history, any science, was far inferior to that of the people of Rome five hundred years earlier. Most of the good books of Greece and Rome had been lost or tucked away in chilly monasteries.

Harun's civilization was, by comparison, rich and sumptuous. So rich was Harun's court that his wife Zubaydah would use only vessels of gold and silver on her table, and she ornamented her shoes with precious stones. On one pilgrimage to Mecca Zubaydah spent three million dinars to bring in water for all Mecca from a fresh spring twenty-five miles away. Harun sent Charlemagne an elephant and a clepsydra, a wonderful water clock. He might have sent books, but most Franks, including Charlemagne himself, did not know how to read.

Harun's caliphate represented a high in culture and a high in bloodshed. It ended in a civil war that caused the destruction of the round city within Baghdad. But when the seventh caliph, al-Mamun, marched into the ruins of Baghdad in 819 and took up residence in the Jafari palace that had been built for a vizier, the all-time-high period of Greek influence on Islamic science began. Al-Mamun believed that the words of the Koran should be interpreted to agree with the judgments of reason— the peripatetic view bemoaned by the strict interpreters of the word of the Book. Al-Mamun dreamed of Aristotle one night, and the old Greek told him there was no difference between reason and the religious law. Thus over the complaints of the conservatives, al-Mamun justified the Bayt al-Hikmah, or House of Learning, which was to Baghdad what the old museum and library had been to Alexandria—a combination of library, college, and translation office.

The Arab empire sent wheat, barley, and rice along the paved roads to Baghdad from the irrigated river valleys. Silver came from the Hindu Kush, where 10,000 miners labored for the caliph. Gold came in from Nubia and the Sudan, copper from Isfahan, and iron from Sicily. Timber was shipped by sailing boat from the western regions. Harun's engineers were forever draining swamps. They built factories to make goods and carpets. They manufactured silk, a process learned from China. They made linen in Egypt. They made paper, another Chinese product. They made fine pottery, metal jewelry, soap and perfumes for use in the public baths.

At this time, one of the major cultural differences between East and West was the matter of emphasis. Great books existed in the West, in Byzantium in particular, but the focus of interest in Western Europe was almost totally religious. The Churches in Rome and Byzantium demanded that man worry only about his soul and be devoted to God. In the Arab empire men were free to inquire. Islam had just as strict religionists as Europe, but they were not in the ascendant as they were in Europe. So Islam's scientific interest sparkled, while Europe's was dead.

By this time Arab scientists had begun to classify the studies of science under what is called the Farabi system, five classifications. This system indicates how the Muslims regarded the processes of higher learning.

First in the Arab approach came the science of language, natural enough, because of the need for perfecting the language to carry the ideas of science. Among the studies here were syntax, grammar, pronunciation, and speech and poetry. Poetry has continued to occupy a high post in Islam.

Second came logic, based on the writings of the Greeks.

Third came the propaedeutic (that is, preparatory or introductory) sciences: arithmetic; geometry; optics; the science of the heavens, including astrology; music; the science of weights; the science of tool making.

Fourth came physics and metaphysics. Physics included knowledge of the principles which underlie natural bodies and the principle of their combination, elements, compounds, minerals, plants.

Metaphysics included knowledge of the essence of beings, the principles of the particular and observational sciences, and knowledge of noncorporeal beings "which would lead finally to the knowledge of God."

Fifth and last came the science of society, which included jurisprudence and rhetoric.

By modern definition not all these are sciences, but to Islam such distinctions held no importance The historian Seyyed Hossein Nasr offered an interesting theory that Arabs encouraged the systematic study of the body of Greek knowledge because of the challenge posed by the religious minorities within the empire, particularly the Christians and Jews. In the debates that were often carried on among religious groups in the big cities, the Muslims often "lost" because they could not defend themselves with the same logic that the Christians and

Jews used. Thus, says Nasr, since the caliphate was based
on religious law, it had a definite interest in proving that
the way of Islam was the proper way.

The system of scientific education was also changing.
The first caliphs ruled through religion. In the mosques
of the cities, narrators recited the Koran and told the
faithful the legends and traditions of Islam. These narrators developed into language teachers, and when written language became used generally, they were the in-
structors in grammar and literature. From this point,
developed the elementary schools or *maktub*. Most students got no further than the maktub, but a few might
go on to special training in reading, writing, and religion.
By the ninth century another form of school had come
into being: the *majlis*, or circle. It was headed by a pro-
fessor, called a *hakim* (wise man). He was a scholar and
spiritual guide who might even be a physician.

After study with the hakim, the young scholar was on
his own. He might seek further instruction at a medical
college and hospital such as Jundishapur, or he might
apprentice himself to a scholar.

By the end of the eighth century many scholars had
flocked to Baghdad to enjoy the freedom and support of
the caliphate.

The ninth century opened then on a state of affairs
that was to persist in the scientific life of Islam.

The Arabs tended to concern themselves with matters
of Islamic history, language, and theology. Most of the
students were non-Arabs.

In fact, the leader of the caliph's translators, Hunayn
ibn-Ishak, was a Christian physician. He had been dis-
penser to a great physician named ibn-Masawayh, had

left that post and studied Greek, and so was sent
west to search out Greek manuscripts. Coming back to
the caliphate, he entered the service of Jibril ibn-Bakh-
tishu, physician to Caliph al-Mumun, and came to the
attention of the caliph and was made head of the House
of Learning.

No better man could have been chosen. Because of his
experience, he knew good manuscripts from fakes. He
spent much time comparing and then supervising translation. Often it was very complicated, as with Aristotle's
works. Hunayn would put a work into Syriac, and his
son Ishak translated it into Arabic.

Hunayn and his men translated Hippocrates and Dioscorides, the first-century Greek physician. They translated Plato's *Republic* and much of Aristotle. Most important, they translated nearly all of Galen's works, for
seven of the Galen books on anatomy which they translated into Arabic were later lost in the original Greek.
Centuries later, when Europe's intellectual interest began
to revive, all that was left were the Arabic translations.

The typical pay for a translation was 500 dinars a
month, but when Hunayn worked for the caliph, he and
his assistants received the weight in gold of the books
they translated. Thus Hunayn became a rich man and
lived very well. He arose early in the morning and went
for a horseback ride, then repaired to the public bath for
refreshment. After his bath, he put on a robe and had
breakfast, then lay down for a nap. After the nap, he
steeped himself in incense and then ate his midday meal,
usually soup, chicken, and bread. After lunch he took
another nap and on waking drank some wine, perhaps
flavored with quinces and apples.

But not all life was so easy even for a favorite of the caliph. At one time, when Hunayn fell out of favor with the caliph, he was imprisoned for an entire year. His crime was that he would not prepare a poison for an enemy of the caliph. At the end of the year Hunayn was brought again before the caliph and threatened with death. Again he refused. Why? asked the caliph, as the headsman tested his ax. Because his Christian religion decreed that he should do good unto his enemies, and his profession limited him to work for the benefit of mankind, said Hunayn. He was under oath never to give anyone a deadly medicine.

Since the caliph could find other poisoners but might not find so good a physician to treat his gout or a man of intellect to lead his translators, Hunayn was freed and went back to work. He lived a long time, and before he died, he established in the House of Learning the foundation of all Muslim knowledge of medicine.

Arab medicine began with the Persian school at Jundishapur. The first Arab physician of the scientific school was al-Harith ibn-Kaladah, a contemporary of the prophet Muhammad, who attended Jundishapur in the seventh century. Little attention was paid in Mecca to al-Harith, however, because the Arabs of Mecca and Medina preferred the folk medicine they knew best, which had come from the civilization to the south of Hejaz. Therefore, although al-Harith had studied at the Persian college and hospital at Jundishapur, there was no flocking of students from the Arab peninsula to follow.

Instead, the faithful gathered together the sayings of the Prophet regarding medical treatment, hygiene, and diet, and the old folk medicine continued to be the guide for the Arabs for many years after the death of the Prophet. The *imam*, the man who led the faithful in prayer and also led them in war, was not an unlikely candidate to practice medicine in the desert, because he represented that wedding of religious, political, and cultural life that characterized the nature of Islam. The *hakim*, the educated man of Islam, was to be known as physician, philosopher, and usually also as linguist and scientist. The sixth Shiite imam, for example, Jafar al-Sadiq, was equally well known in Islam as imam and as compiler of a book of the medical observations of the Prophet.

Still, Jundishapur was the place where Islamic scholars soon learned a more rational basis for medical practice.

Jundishapur, near the present Persian city of Ahwaz, goes back to the old Fertile Crescent days as a place of civilized learning. In those times it was called the Beautiful Garden. The garden fell with the changing of the civilizations, but the city had been rebuilt in the third century A.D. by Shapur I, the second king of the Persian Sassanid empire, and that is how the city got its name.

In the early contact between the Greeks and Persians, Jundishapur became a center of Greek learning, particularly of the Hippocratic doctrine of medicine. In A.D. 489, the Byzantine emperor had closed down the medical school at Edessa in a religious dispute, and the dissident priest-teacher-physicians took refuge with the Persians at Jundishapur. Soon Shapur II built a university there. The Greek influence was strengthened in 529 when the medical school at Athens was closed and the teachers also fled to Persia.

During the sixth century, the Persian emperor Anushi-rawan sent officials to India to learn the Indian sciences, among them Burzuyah, his vizir. Burzuyah came back with several Indian physicians. Shortly afterwards he wrote down a statement of the Persian tradition, now guided by Greek and Indian ways.

> I exerted myself in the treatment of patients whom I expected to cure. And no less did I strive in those cases where I could not hope to effect a cure. In such cases I tried at least to make their sufferings more bearable. Whenever I could I used to attend in person to my cases. When this was impossible I would write out for them the necessary prescriptions and give them medicines. From no one whom I treated did I demand a fee or any sort of reward. And none of my colleagues did I envy who equalled me in knowledge and surpassed me in fame or fortune, if he was lax in his standards of honesty or in word or deed.

So when the Arabs conquered Persia in the seventh century, they came upon this well-developed medical center, and they did not disturb it.

After Caliph al-Mansur took Jirjis ibn-Bakhtyashu to Baghdad to treat the caliph's dyspepsia, soon another physician named Masawai came to Baghdad, where he became a famous ophthalmologist and the physician to Harun al-Rashid. He had three sons, and all of them became doctors. Yuhanna ibn-Masawai wrote the first Arabic treatise on ophthalmology, a work that represents the first original Arabic work in medicine. This doctor, also known to history as Johannes Damascenus, wrote many works on dietetics and gynecology, too. Another

famed translator, Hunayn ibn-Ishaq, was the best-known
physician of early Baghdad, and he left a textbook on
medicine in the form of questions and answers *(Quaes-
tiones Medicinae)* and ten dissertations on the eye, written in Arabic.

Abdullah ibn-al-Muqaffa translated books from the
Pahlavi of the eastern lands into Arabic, and he was followed by the Indian physician Mikna, who was hired by
Yahya of the Parmacid family to translate medical works.
But the tradition was so much more largely Greek that
the Indian and Persian of the past were submerged in this
period.

Of the original works of this first period of Arabic
medicine, the most important was that of Yuhanna ibn-
Sarabium (Serapion in the West). He was a Syrian Christian who wrote in this time, and his works were quickly
translated into Arabic. His major work was *Aphorisms*
in twelve books. He also wrote a *Pandectae*. And Ali
ibn-Rabban al-Tabari, a Persian convert from Christianity to Islam, wrote a medical encyclopedia called
The Paradise of Wisdom.

So the first period of Arabic medicine came to a close
in about 900, and by the end of it, the Arab students
of medicine had at their fingertips the vast store of
knowledge of the past, both East and West. Indeed, al-
Tabari's encyclopedia was a summation of this knowledge, particularly in the fields of pathology, diet, and
pharmacology, which under the Arabs was to become
very highly developed.

The first period of Arabic medicine ended with the
Muslims in full control of the European and Indian traditions, including the Galenic contributions of the ana-

tomical and experimental ideas. However, because religious regulations prevented the dissection of human bodies, the study of anatomy languished.

The second period of the medicine of eastern Islam is typified by Abu Bakr Muhammed ibn-Zakariyya, usually known to Europeans as Rhazes. He lived between 865 and 923, and was a student of the great al-Tabari at the Baghdad medical school. After learning his profession, Rhazes became a physician at the hospital in his native city of Rai, and later director of that hospital. One hospital had been founded at Baghdad by Harun al-Rashid, following the model of Jundishapur. Rhazes helped found the new hospital that was erected by Caliph al-Maktadir.

In the early days of Rhazes' medical practice, many Arab physicians attached great importance to examination of the urine of patients. They said they could thus diagnose disease without ever seeing the patient. Rhazes knew this claim was not true, and he began to prove it.

One of Rhazes' cases in proof was that of a patient named Abdullah ibn-Sawads, who came to the hospital suffering from attacks of fever, occurring sometimes every day and then sometimes every six days. The other doctors examined the patient's urine, but they had no idea what was wrong with him, even after they found evidence of infection.

Rhazes saw the patient and treated him in a way that would be approved in modern medicine. Hearing the symptoms, he said the patient might be suffering from an ulceration of the kidneys. He treated Abdullah with diuretics until the signs of infection began to disappear, and then treated him with other drugs, until in two months the ulcer was cured. All the while, the other physicians had no idea of the cause of Abdullah's illness. The reason, of course, was that Rhazes was following the Hippocratic tradition and not the magical traditions that sometimes overwhelmed some of the Arab doctors.

Rhazes was also capable of using a high degree of psychology in his treatment of the nobility (and it seems that this was essential to the physician who would keep his head under the fierce Abbasids).

One day Rhazes was called upon to treat the Emir (Governor or Under King) Mansur ibn-Muh ibn-Nasr, of the house of Saman, who lived beyond the Oxus River. Rhazes and his servant rode to the shores of the Oxus, but then Rhazes refused to get into the boat provided by Emir Mansur's men. Instead he sent directions for the treatment of the emir and a copy of his latest book, saying that these would do as well as he. But when the emir received this word, he was furious. He sent back more men, with a thousand dinars and one of his own private horses. Rhazes still would not get into the boat, so the soldiers bound him and carried him in. Then they set him free on the other side of the Oxus, and he rode the horse to the court of the emir.

At the court in Bukhara, Rhazes began the treatment of the haughty emir but did no good. Apparently the nobleman was suffering from hysterical paralysis. But this would be no excuse for Rhazes if he failed, and he knew his life was in danger. He went before the emir and told him that he was going to try another treatment but that he must have a horse and a mule to sacrifice. He chose two specific animals known for their speed and endurance.

The emir put these beasts at Rhazes' disposal. Next

day, Rhazes took the emir to the hot springs at Juyi
Muliyan outside the palace. He also had his servant bring
the horse and mule to the outside of the baths and have
them ready. Then he took the emir into the baths and
locked the door so none of the courtiers or servants could
get in. He gave the emir a bath and made him drink the
tepid water. But that did no good either. The emir was
paralyzed.

Then Rhazes put on his clothes and took a knife in
his hand. He stood before the paralyzed emir, waving
the knife and threatening him.

"Thou didst order thy people to bind and cast me into
the boat and threaten my life. If I do not destroy thee as
a punishment for this, I am no true son of [my father]
Zakariyya."

The emir was not used to being threatened by his subjects. He was furious and managed painfully to get up
onto his knees. Rhazes waved the knife and threatened
him again. The emir was purple with rage. He stood up.

When Rhazes saw the emir stand up, he turned and
ran out of the room. He jumped on the horse and his
servant jumped on the mule. They did not stop until
they had crossed the Oxus and reached the town of
Merv on the other side. Then Rhazes sat down and wrote
a letter to the emir.

> May the life of the King be prolonged in health of body
> and effective command. I, your servant, undertook the
> treatment and did all that was possible. There was,
> however, an extreme failure in the natural caloric, and
> the treatment of the disease would have been a protracted
> affair. I therefore abandoned it in favor of a physical
> treatment, carried you to the hot bath, administered a

draught, and left you so long as to bring about a coction [digestion] of the humours. Then I angered the King, so as to aid the natural caloric, and it gained strength until those humours, already softened, were dissolved. But henceforth it is not expedient that a meeting should take place between myself and the king.

When the emir received that letter, he already knew what had happened. He had stood up to chastise this hateful physician, but when Rhazes had run out the door, the emir had fainted. Then he came to his senses, got up, and walked out of the bath unaided, asking where the doctor had gone. He went back to his palace and gave an audience to the courtiers. The people saw that the emir was well again and rejoiced. They searched for Rhazes and could not find him. But seven days later the servant arrived with the letter, the mule, and the horse. The emir sent Rhazes a horse with full equipment, a cloak, turban, arms, a slave boy and a slave girl, and assigned to him a yearly allowance of 2,000 dinars and 200 loads of corn.

However, dealing with the nobility was not always so easy, and it was reported that a member of this same Mansur family of Bukhara became displeased when Rhazes failed to carry out some chemical experiment he had described in a book. The emir ordered Rhazes beaten on the head with his book until the book or the head broke. And thus Rhazes was blinded.

But before this great physician-scientist lost his sight, he accomplished a great deal, and before he died, he accomplished more. He developed the use of animal gut in sutures. He introduced mercurial ointment for diseases of the skin and eyes and other medicines. He added to the knowledge of anatomy. His book on smallpox was completely original, based on his experience as a physician, and he was the first to differentiate between this disease and lesser spotting diseases such as measles. In other words, he isolated the disease and offered a partially effective treatment for the first time.

> The eruption of the Small Pox [he wrote] is preceded by a continued fever, pain in the back, itching in the nose, and terrors in sleep. These are the more peculiar symptoms of its approach, especially a pain in the back, with fever; then also a pricking which the patient feels all over his body, a fullness of the face, which at times goes and comes, and inflamed color, and violent redness in both cheeks, a redness of both the eyes, a heaviness of the whole body, great uneasiness, the symptoms of which are stretching and yawning; a pain in the throat and chest, with a slight difficulty in breathing, and cough; a dryness of the mouth, thick spittle, and hoarseness of the voice; pain and heaviness of the head, inquietude, distress of the mind, nausea and anxiety; (with this difference that the inquietude, nausea and anxiety are more frequent in the measles than in the small pox, while on the other hand, the pain in the back is more peculiar to the small pox than to the measles;) heat of the whole body, and inflamed color and shining redness, and especially an intense redness of the gums.

The most important of Rhazes' works, however, was his *al-Hawi,* which came down to the west as *Liber Continens.* It was an encyclopedia of practical medicine, which included all the knowledge of the Muslim world of medicines at the beginning of the tenth century. Rhazes died, apparently in poverty, before the book was completed, and it was finished by his students. A physician of the next generation, commenting on it, said it was too voluminous and too expensive for the doctors of Araby. But this critic also said that he found the book discussed everything necessary to the medical man concerning hygiene and medical treatment of known disease. The book became a classic in Arabic medical literature and later, between the twelfth and seventeenth centuries, was highly regarded in the West.

Finally, in this golden period of Abbasid medicine in the tenth century, there was the physician Abu Ali al-Hussein ibn-Abdallah ibn-Sina, known to Europeans as Avicenna. He was born in a small town near Bukhara around A.D. 980, and went to a traditional mosque school, where he learned the Koran by heart by the time he was ten years old. He then studied Aristotle, grammar, dialetics, astronomy, geometry, and finally medicine.

Ibn-Sina was obviously a child prodigy, for at ten the Koran was not enough—he also knew so much about Arabic and Persian literature that his name was known throughout Transoxiana, where he lived.

As a youth, studying philosophy, he outstripped his teacher. He took up mathematics, and studied the first five propositions of Euclid under a master, then worked out the rest of them himself. It was then that ibn-Sina began the study of medicine, and here is what he had to say about it himself, a book written about his youthful life:

> Medicine is not a difficult subject, and in a short space of time, of course, I excelled in it, so that the master of physic came to read with me, and I began to visit the sick. Consequently there were opened to me the doors to

various kinds of treatment which I learnt by experience
(or experiment). I was then about sixteen years of age.
During the period of hard practice and study which then
ensued, I never once slept the whole night through. If a
problem was too great for me, I repaired to the mosque
and prayed, invoking the Creator of all things, until the
gate that had been closed to me was opened and what
had been complex became simple. Always, as night fell,
I returned to my house, set the lamp before me and
busied myself with reading and writing. If sleep overcame
me or I felt the flesh growing weak, I had recourse to a
beaker of wine, so that my energies were restored. . . .*

So ibn-Sina began the practice of medicine and prospered. Like Rhazes he had his difficulties with the harsh
and demanding rulers. One day, when he was at the
court of the Khwarizm Shah, ruler of Khiva, a message
came from a famous warrior named Mahmud of Ghazna,
demanding the presence immediately of Ibn-Sina and
other learned men. A refusal was dangerous, but an ac-
ceptance might be too—for who knew what problem
this unlettered warrior would put before the council of
learned men?—who knew what he might do if they
failed to solve this problem? It was a day when rulers
readily lopped off the heads of those who pretended
learning but failed in a practical showing of their
prowess.

Ibn-Sina decided to decline, and the decision taken,
his host the Khwarizm Shah helped him escape to the
city of Gurgan on the shore of the Caspian Sea, until

---

* In spite of the Islamic prohibition against liquor, many Muslims
continued to drink wine and spirits.

Mahmud might have forgotten the sting of the young physician's refusal.

Ibn-Sina's family was of the upper class. His father had been a tax collector, no mean responsibility in the Abbasid empire, and ibn-Sina had been taught that the way of success lay through government service. In addition to his medical and scientific studies he had studied philosophy with a learned man, Natili, renowned in his own time, and he had also studied jurisprudence. With all these qualifications, then, ibn-Sina sought various political jobs to support himself, and secured them, one after another. For a time he was vizier, or prime minister, to the emir of Hamadan. Here he engaged in religious argument with the strict believers of the army, and they called for his execution. Soldiers came to his house, searching for him, and when they did not find the vizier, they plundered the house and then called on the emir to cut off his head. Ibn-Sina was warned in time and fled into hiding once again, this time at the home of his friend Abu Said Dafdaq. While in seclusion he worked on his *Canon*. Then one day the emir of Hamadan fell ill and called for ibn-Sina to come and treat him. The physician came, cured the emir, and was restored to favor, once again showing how slender a thread held the lives of those who sought greatness in the Abbasid empire. Had ibn-Sina failed to cure the emir, even though no fault of his own, the course of his life might either have run out or been changed. For some time now, ibn-Sina was to have perfect freedom in which to work. He worked on the *Canon* and on the *Shifa,* which was a compendium of the principles of metaphysics, philosophy, and logic.

In this period of intensive intellectual activity, one has a view of the manner in which ibn-Sina and the favored intellectuals of the Baghdad caliphate were allowed to live. Each evening his students would come to the house, and he would read to them the work he had accomplished during the day, and they would discuss the work in a seminar fashion. Then there would be dinner and wine and entertainment for the host and his guests.

After several years the emir of Hamadan died. Once again ibn-Sina's future was uncertain. The new emir wanted him to remain in his service, but the relationship would have to be established all over again, and ibn-Sina for reasons of his own feared for his life if he remained in Hamadan. Again he escaped, helped by friends, and traveled to Isfahan disguised as dervish, or wandering Muslim holy man. Again he went to work on his *Canon*. He remained there for the rest of his productive life, and died in 1037, while on the way from Isfahan back to Hamadan.

The medicine of ibn-Sina's day, based on the old Greek and Roman beliefs, stemmed from the concept that the whole physical world was composed of four elements: earth, air, fire, and water. But also there were four qualities of nature to affect these elements: heat, cold, dryness, and wetness. Each element had one or more of the qualities. It might be hot and moist, or hot and dry. Or it might just be characterized as cold, or simply as wet. Everything on earth was some kind of mixture of elements and qualities.

This theory led to the further theory of the *humors* mentioned earlier. These were said to govern the condition of the human body. The humors were also four in

number: black bile, blood, yellow bile, and phlegm, all
present in the body. Health and disposition depended
on the combination and strength of the humors at any
given time, and general character was credited to a pre-
ponderance of one humor over another. For example, a
man with much black bile would have a great deal of
hair on his chest and be gloomy by nature. Too much
yellow bile, and the mixture made a man quick-tem-
pered. Too much phlegm made him slow and phlegmatic.

Humors were produced by food, said the Arabic
theorists, beginning when it first went into digestion
(coction) in the stomach. It was divided into three parts:
chyle, the most nutritious, which is the juice extracted,
excreta, and phlegm. The chyle went to the liver, carried
by the portal vein, and there a second digestion took
place, separating the substance into three parts. First
was a froth which was yellow bile. Second was a sedi-
ment: black bile. Third was blood, which contained the
choice ingredients of the food. The blood went to the
heart and then to the arteries, where there was a third
digestion. Then the blood went to various parts of the
body, each of which digested its little bit.

That was the physical theory of man's being, but it
did not represent all of Arab belief. There was also the
matter of man's place in the universe. Man was born and
lived under the influence of the planets and stars. And
so a physician had to be philosopher and astrologer to a
certain degree.

Ibn-Sina has been called the most famous scientist of
Islam, because he was far more than a physician. His important work, *Canon of Medicine,* was a philosophical
and factual treatise on medicine, including descriptions
of a number of diseases, the consideration of 760 drugs,

an outline of pharmacology. His work became *the* authoritative source for Islamic medicine. One writer of Islam, in evaluating the book, said that if a doctor had mastered the first volume of ibn-Sina's *Canon* by the time he was forty years old, he would be "worthy of confidence."

In Islamic medicine, then, the student of the eleventh and twelfth centuries began with Hippocrates' *Aphorisms,* went on to the *Questions* of Hunayn ibn-Ishaq, to the *Book of al-Mansur* of Rhazes, then the works of Galen, and finally to the *Canon* of ibn-Sina. If he mastered all these, he was considered an extremely learned man in the arts of medicine—and this attitude prevailed in Islam until the twentieth century.

One peculiar aspect of Arabic medicine was its administration by an official called the *muhtasib,* who was responsible directly to the caliph. The muhtasib was more than a health officer, he was also a superintendent of public morality, and it was his task to see that the doctors neither cheated the people nor offended against the tenets of the Koran.

Medicine was classified, then as now, as both science and art. Its justification under the laws of the Koran was in the medical function of conserving the health of the body. The muhtasib was responsible for seeing that those who practiced medicine knew their art and science. He made them take the Hippocratic oath, basically the same oath taken by physicians in the modern world. They swore never to administer medicines to make anyone sick, to poison a person, or to bring about abortion or prevent conception. They must not reveal confidences.

The medical schools of the caliphate did not give

formal degrees, but to practice in Baghdad the candidate
must satisfy the muhtasib that he could practice medicine. A youth might apprentice himself to a physician,
but when he was ready to practice he had to undergo an
examination. An eye doctor, for example, had to show
familiarity with Hunayn ibn-Ishaq's *Ten Discourses on
the Eye*, a valuable work which dealt with the structures
of the eye, and treatment and remedies for diseases. They
all had to show the muhtasib that they could use the
instruments and remedies, such as lancets for bleeding,
kohl or antimony, and a hook that was used to remove
growths inside the conjunctiva.

Those who would set broken bones must show that
they knew their anatomy and were familiar with every
bone in the body (the number being put by the Arabs
at 248).

Below the position of physicians were surgeons, cuppers, and phlebotomists (bloodletters). Surgeons were
required to know their Galen and later their ibn-Sina.
Specifically they must be familiar with the chapters on
wounds and dressings, with anatomy, and especially the
blood vessels, muscles, and ligaments. They must display
their instruments, and the collection must include speci-
fied numbers and types of lancets, knives, a hatchet to
break the skull, an amputating saw, an eardrum piercer,
leeches, dressings, and certain standard medicines.

Cuppers would scrape the skin and then apply vacuum
pressure by using cups to bring the blood to the surface.
They had to know anatomy so that they would not destroy vital tissues as they worked.

An important medical functionary was the phlebotomist, or bleeder. Up until very nearly modern times,

doctors practiced venesection, bloodletting of patients, for the treatment of a number of diseases (mostly fevers), in the belief that it was a curative measure. In Araby those who would be phlebotomists had to practice on the veins of beet leaves before they touched animals or humans. Phlebotomy was strictly regulated, because of the dangers of murder by unscrupulous practitioners in the pay of heirs. Bleeding had to be done in public. No slave could be bled without his master's permission, no minor without permission of his guardian. The veins that might be bled were listed, so many on the head, so many in the body, hands, and feet. The phlebotomist was also the circumciser of Islam, and the equipment and conditions of this operation were specifically described in the manual of the muhtasib.

The physician was not so different a man from the modern-day doctor, nor were his relations with patients unlike those of the twentieth century, as is indicated in some advice given by one of the Baghdad nobility to his son.

> Once you embark on a career as a physician, if you wish to gain experience and a reputation you must experiment freely, but you had better not choose people of high rank or political importance for your subjects. To gain competence, you must see a great deal of service in hospitals, where cases of all sorts pass under your hands, and where you should actually see for yourself what you have read about in the textbooks. With such training, no disease, however rare, will present you with any difficulty and diseases of the internal organs will be no mystery to you.

When you visit a patient in his house, you must be clean in person and dress and agreeably perfumed. The expression of your countenance should be pleasant and you should go only when you are untroubled in spirit. The physician's encouraging words increase the potency of the warmth inherent in a man's natural temperament. Never try to cover your failures by charging the patient with not having obeyed your instructions. . . .

One might say, then, that Arabic medicine was sophisticated for its times and far ahead of that of the rest of the world. By the second half of the ninth century, under Rhazes, medicine was making large strides, both in treatment and in the scholarly approach to theory. Rhazes was the greatest clinician of Islam and of all the Middle Ages, and Hunayn ibn-Ishaq was the greatest translator. In the first half of the tenth century, the physicians of Islam were publishing the important new ideas. In the second half of that century the medicine of Islam had become very complex, and was divided into three areas, all slightly different: that of Baghdad, that of Egypt, and that of Muslim Spain. (The last two will be discussed separately.)

The eleventh century brought the medicine of Baghdad to its zenith, with ibn-Sina's works. From that time on the medicine of the eastern Muslim world remained largely as it was.

7

The Decline of
the Abbasids

THE ARABS had been the first to make science international, and one of the principal factors in this extension was also of vast importance in the development of "the exact sciences," which in those times meant arithmetic, geometry, astronomy, and music. The factor was the nature of the Arabic language.

That language is made up of 3,726 basic words, each containing three consonants. Differences in meaning are expressed by changing inflection and vowel sounds within the three consonants. Arabic lends itself, thus, to terse expression, which is just what is wanted by mathematicians and astronomers in particular. The Arabic language is particularly suitable for expression of scientific concepts and for developing them, because the language flows without connectives.

Early, the science of astronomy had begun to make some strides at the school in Jundishapur, which already had a tradition of mixed Indian-Greek knowledge. The Muslims were very much interested in the study of the stars because of the need for finding the way to Mecca and regularizing the hours of prayer, and the beginnings and ends of the special months such as Ramadan, the month of fasting.

In the House of Learning in Baghdad, while the translators were working, and the great al-Kindi (Abu Yusuf Yaqub ibn-al-Sabbah al-Kindi) was studying Aristotle and developing his own philosophy, the mathematicians and astronomers began to work, too. The three sons of the noble Musa ibn-Shakir devoted their lives and fortunes to science. They hired translators (Hunayn ibn-Ishaq among them), and they are credited with original writings. Abu Jaffar was a student of Euclid, Ahmad was interested in mechanics, Hasan's specialty was geometry. They wrote a book on the balance, and one dealing with the measurement of the sphere. They studied the trisection of the angle and other mathematical problems.

Caliph al-Mamun built observatories. The first of these seems to be the one called the Shammasiya Observatory at Baghdad. One of the principal astronomers was Yahy ibn-abi-Mansur, who was also attached to the House of Learning. At the same time, al-Mamun established another observatory, the Qasiyun Observatory at Damascus, and the observations of these two were simultaneous, at least sometimes.

During the reign of al-Mamun a party of astronomers and artisans was sent to the observatory near Tadmor (ancient Palmyra) to make measurements of the altitude of the sun and to divide the earth into its 360 degrees, measure them, and determine the circumference of the earth. Another party went to Sanjar in Persia to do the same. They found the degree to be 56⅔ miles, the earth to be 20,400 miles around, agreeing with Ptolemy.

He and they were way off, of course. The earth's circumference at the equator is estimated by modern geodesists at 24,901.55 statute miles, and a degree of latitude varies in length from 68.708 miles there to 69.403

at the poles. It was by following Ptolemy's miscalcula-
tion of the earth's size that Christopher Columbus was
led to believe he'd encountered the East Indies only three
thousand miles west of Spain. However, the remarkable
thing is that the second-century Greek and the ninth-
century Arabs had undertaken such a determination at
all.

The most important early figure in astronomy and
mathematics was Abu Abdullah Muhammed ibn-Musa
al-Khwarizmi, born at Khwarizm near the Aral Sea. He
was a mathematician, astronomer, and geographer, and
it was said that he supervised some of the stargazing at
the observatories of al-Mamun, although he was not
regularly engaged in this work.

Persia had an astronomical and mathematical tradition dating from the Sassanids, the last Persian emperors.
Then, when Mumad al-Fazari was official astronomer to
the Abbasid dynasty, in the 770s, an Indian mission had
come to Baghdad to teach the Muslims science. Al-
Khwarizmi was responsible for bringing all this knowledge together. He also worked with the Hindu numerals,
and developed algebra, which comes from the Arabic
word *al-jabr,* which means reduction of the parts to a
whole, or the reunion of broken parts. He made analyti-
cal solutions of linear and quadratic equations. In other
words, he founded algebra as a science separate from
geometry.

To understand how this branch of mathematics works,
take a simple problem: the determination of a right triangle. The ancient Egyptians determined a triangle by
measurement. They found that if a triangle had sides
of the length 3, 4, and 5, then it was a right triangle with

a right angle opposite the longest side. The Greeks, by developing geometry, proved that the square of the hypotenuse (the longest side) was equal to the sum of the squares of the other two. The Arabs, by developing algebra, learned to express the truths thus: $a^2 + b^2 = c^2$.

One mathematical advance that developed out of astronomy was the concept of zero. It's difficult to imagine a mathematician of today being able to handle numbers, especially large ones, without this useful digit. The Babylonians had already devised a place-value system in mathematics—that is, one in which the value of a digit is determined by its position in the written-out number. For example, the value of the digit 5 in the number 357 is not 5 but 50. But suppose a man adds 25 to 15? How is he to indicate an even number unless he has some symbol to place beside the 4? Late in the Babylonian period some unknown astronomer devised such a symbol and employed it henceforth in all celestial calculations.

From the Babylonians, the concept passed to the Greeks, who molded the Babylonian symbol into our familiar 0 and passed it on to the Hindus, and from there it came back again to the Arabs. Their word for zero— *sifr*, "empty"—comes into English as "cipher."

The Babylonians had a sexagesimal system of calculating, employing basic numbers from 1 to 60. This system was still in operation by the time it reached the Arabs, and they continued to employ it in astronomy. However, they simultaneously developed our modern decimal system of basic numbers from 1 to 10.

Al-Khwarizmi also developed astronomical and trigonometric tables, containing the sine function and also the tangent. The sine was discovered to be the perpen-

dicular drawn from one extremity of the arc of a circle
to the diameter drawn through the other extremity. In
modern times it has come to be a kind of mathematical
shorthand, based on the known fact that the sine of any
angle equals the sine of its supplement and is the negative of the sine of the negative angle.

The tangent is a line that meets the curve of a circle
or surface of a sphere at two or more points and thus
has the same general direction as the curve or surface.
In trigonometry the tangent would subtend or measure
the angle, the quotient of the sine divided by the cosine
of the angle.

At this time a number of astronomers became famous
in the Muslim world for their writing on astrology, and
chief of them was Abu Mashar, whose name came down
to the West later as Albumazar. His introduction to
astrology became one of the most widely read works on
the subject.

In this period the caliphate was extending its influence far and wide by trade and raiding parties, and
through these groups some of Arab science, and particularly Arab arithmetic using the Hindu numbers, began spreading around the world. The observational astronomers were at work, too, and skilled instrument
makers were building ever larger instruments, to try to
cut the margins of error in observation.

Those Banu Musa brothers, who had devoted their
lives to science, became interested in astronomy.

Another important astronomer of this period was Abu
Hanifa Ahmad ibn-Dawud ibn-Wanand al-Dinawari,
who lived in Dinawar and Isfahan, making observations
in the former place from the roof of a house. But the

major astronomer of the age, and one of the primary astronomers of any age in history, was Abu Abdullah Mohammed ibn-Jabir ibn-Sinan al-Battani, who lived in the tenth century and made observations at Raqqa in Syria over a period of forty years.

Al-Battani had an astrolabe for use in rough measurements, a gnomon divided into twelve parts, horizontal and vertical sundials, an armillary sphere, and parallactic rulers. He also had a mural quadrant, and an alidade. A gnomon is any upright object by the length of whose shadow the hours of the day or the height of a neighboring object can be determined; the pointer of a sundial is officially a gnomon. Parallax is the apparent displacement of an object seen from two different angles; the difference in what a right eye sees from what the left sees is parallax, and parallactic rulers are devices to measure this displacement difference. A mural quadrant is a quarter circle mounted on a wall for stability and equipped with a movable arm used to measure the altitude angles of celestial bodies. An alidade is a movable arm, as on a quadrant, equipped with sights and used to determine direction or angular height; the name comes from the Arabic *al-idadah,* meaning "the radius of a circle."

Al-Battani amended the findings of Ptolemy and made new findings in the calculations of the orbits of the moon. His main book on astronomy was so impressive that it remained a basic work until the Renaissance of Europe.

One can see, then, that by the tenth century Arabic astronomy and mathematics were becoming very important. So were the observatories as places of record keeping. So were the instruments becoming more complex and accurate.

The depth and range of the work is indicated by this development of observatories and instruments. Abd al-Rahman al-Sufi built a silver celestial globe to represent the heavens for the ruler Adud al-Dawla, at a huge cost.

The Sharaf al-Dawla, who ruled between 982 and 989 built an observatory in the garden of his royal residence in Baghdad. Abu Mahmud Hamid ibn-al-Khidr al-Khujandi built an astrolabe larger than all previous ones constructed in Islam. It consisted of a 60-degree meridian arc with a radius of about twenty meters. Each degree was divided into 360 parts, and each ten-second portion was distinguishable on the scale. The arc was constructed between two walls at a hill called Jabal Tabruk near Rai. It was faced with wood, and sheets of copper were attached to the wood. The ceiling was arched, and the hole in it had a diameter of 2 centimeters and a movable cover slid over the arc.

In astronomy, Ptolemy's work was totally familiar to all competent astronomers, although they had departed from his system in some ways. They created a solar calendar for use in fixing harvests and collecting taxes, although the religious leaders maintained the lunar calendar as a guide to everyday life.

Then came the first half of the eleventh century, which was the high point of Arab mathematics and astronomy, as it was in nearly all the sciences. Mathematicians and astronomers, in the Baghdad caliphate in this period, were doing new work. Kushyar ibn-Labban made new discoveries in trigonometry, Ibn al-Hussain furthered the development of geometry, the mathematician al-

Nasawi wrote a practical book of arithmetic in Persian and then translated it into Arabic. He used decimal fractions. But the most important of these men, as important to the mathematical sciences as ibn-Sina (Avicenna) was to the medical sciences in the period, was Abu Raihan Muhammad ibn-Ahmad al-Biruni. He was born in Khwarizm in 973 and lived for a time in India. He died in 1048. Although we call him an Arab scientist, he was a Persian and a Shiite, and he disliked the caliphate and Arabism in particular. He is regarded as one of the greatest scientists of all time.

Al-Biruni translated several works from the Sanskrit of India. He made a clear study of the Hindu numeral system. He showed how to determine latitudes and longitudes accurately. Like Avicenna, al-Biruni was the "medieval man," concerning himself with all the aspects of life. The hydrostatic principle of physics interested him when he examined some natural springs. He was a geologist. When he visited the Indus Valley, he suggested that it was an ancient sea basin filled with alluvium. Medicine and pathology were his concern when he investigated the phenomenon of Siamese twins.

The Arabs also developed natural history. Around the beginning of the ninth century an Arab born in al-Basrah named Abd al-Malik ibn-Quraib al-Asma'i wrote a number of works on various animals, books which showed a good knowledge of anatomy. In addition to man, he wrote on the horse, the camel, wild animals, and the sheep. In the ninth century, the Muslims had a very good knowledge of minerology and particularly of precious stones. A work on such stones, a lapidary, was written by Utarid. Early in the tenth century ibn-Washiya wrote a study of agriculture which showed an excellent knowledge of agricultural practices. Late in that century al-Tamini wrote a guide toward the understanding of foodstuffs and simple drugs.

The value of works such as these, and the biology studies of the Arabs was partly the revival of Aristotelian knowledge of biology and other subjects. Also in the tenth century there was organized a secret society known as the Brethren of Purity, whose purpose was to reconcile Greek science with the Koran, because these men believed in the purifying power of knowledge. They wrote a number of treatises in an encyclopedic form, dealing with mysticism and with such sciences as zoology, botany, and anthropology.

There were other scientific studies in this period of high renaissance in the Baghdad caliphate. Al-Biruni developed and used the balance, which was a matter of mechanics. Qusta ibn-Luqa translated the works of Heron of Alexandria (on pulleys and their uses).

The Muslims had a lively interest in geography, because of the very nature of their empire and its twin centers in Mecca and Medina. One of the first great geographers was the astronomer and mathematician al-Khwarizmi, who read and improved on Ptolemy's geography, and corrected errors in that Greek scholar's maps of various parts of the world. Soon the Arabs were drawing maps of the world.

One notable traveler of the period was Suleiman the merchant, who journeyed to China several times. Another was ibn-Wahb, who traveled the seas to the East. From these and other voyages came the tales of Sindbad the Sailor. Men of the Baghdad caliphate traveled to the lands of Andalusia, North Africa, southern Europe, and Asia. They sailed the Indian Ocean and all the seas around it, using specially built astrolabes for navigation.

In the ninth century ibn-Khurdadhibih, the director of the post office, made the first study of the roads and major geographical features of the provinces of the empire in his *Book of Roads and Provinces,* which came down as a very important source of information on the historical topography of the caliphate. Al-Yaqubi wrote a *Book of the Countries,* which contained much material about geographical features and the economics of the empire. He also wrote a history of the world down to 872, the first part dealing with the world from creation to the time of Islam, and the second concerned with the history of Islam.

In the first half of the tenth century geographer ibn-Serapion wrote a book particularly notable for its detail about the Euphrates, the Tigris, and the Nile rivers. He described the canals of Baghdad with such detail that it was later possible to reconstruct the city.

Abu Zaid wrote the most comprehensive account of Chinese geography available to the West until the time of Marco Polo. Ibn-Fadlan wrote about the far lands known now as Russia and described the geography and people he met on travels there. Abu Dulaf wrote on a trip he took across southern India and through Tibet. Al-Masudi wrote on many travels and "gave fine descriptions of what he saw and heard about, from earthquakes to windmills." Midway in the tenth century, al-Istakhri revised earlier works and created a book which contained colored maps for every known country in the world. His work was in turn revised at his own request in the tenth century by ibn-Hawqal, who had traveled widely through the empire, indicating how swiftly the Arab world was bringing its data up to date.

The people of the empire were traveling everywhere. al-Muqaddasi in his century visited nearly every land of Islam. Ibrahim ibn-Yaqub, a Jewish merchant and traveler, went to Germany and visited the court of Otto I at Magdeburg. Then he went into the Slavic countries.

In the matter of history, the Arabs began very early to adopt a factual approach. Historiography begins with the works on the Arab conquests written by ibn-Abd al-Makam about Egypt and North Africa and Spain, and those of Ahmad ibn-Yahya al-Baladhuri, who integrated all the tales of the conquests into one narrative before the beginning of the tenth century.

Muslim history was written in the words of eyewitnesses, and the historians insisted on dating events to the month and day. They did not devote their efforts to analysis or criticism.

The two great historians of the Abbasid period were Abu Jafar Muhammad ibn-Jarir al-Tabari and Abu al-Hasan Ali al-Masudi.

Al-Tabari's history became a standard reference work for other historians since he arranged his events chronologically, starting with creation and going to A.H. 302. (Among Muslims, time is measured in years "after the Hegira," the flight of Mohammed from Mecca to Medina in A.D. 622. By Christian reckoning, this book covers events up to A.D. 915.) He traveled to Persia, Iraq, Syria, and Egypt. He wrote voluminously—some said forty sheets every single day for forty years.

Al-Masudi, the other great historian of the period,

was sometimes known as the Herodotus of the Arabs. He wrote using the topical method, telling his story through the tales of dynasties and the people. He used historical anecdotes in his work, and he was the first major Arabic historian to go beyond the Muslim world, writing of Indo-Persian, Jewish, and even Roman history.

In history and in the sciences, then, it is apparent that by the middle of the eleventh century, Islam had achieved a higher scientific civilization than the world has generally realized until recent years. The old saw that until the time of Columbus men thought the earth was flat still persists, but in Baghdad five hundred years before Columbus, men not only knew the spherical nature of the earth (as did the Greeks) but had some notion of its vast size. But in this golden age of Arab science dark clouds were already looming on the horizon.

The middle of the eleventh century found the Abbasid caliphate at the height of its glory. The caliph was almost a god, ruling through his vizier, who had complete power over the realm. As Caliph al-Nasir put it at the end of the twelfth century, he who obeyed the vizier obeyed the caliph and thus God, and would go to paradise; he who disobeyed the vizier disobeyed the caliph and disobeyed God, and he would go to hell. For, no matter what else it was, the caliphate was still a religious kingdom, a fact vital to the course of science in the empire. Eventually, science and religion would clash.

That clash would darken the skies above Araby for the next seven hundred years and would eventually contribute to the empire's fall. To know why one must understand the nature of the Arab social system.

In fact, by A.D. 1000 there were three Arab empires.

The Abbasids concentrated their power in the eastern and southern portion of the empire—Arabia itself, Persia, Iraq. The middle section, represented by Syria and Egypt, they allowed to drift into other hands. Farther west, the North African and Spanish Arab empire was even further removed in all ways from the Abbasid seat of power. There was much scientific interchange because of the common language. But as for politics, a Baghdad scientist caught in Granada might be killed as an enemy agent, and the same applied to Spanish or Persian Arabs in Cairo.

One redeeming virtue of the Baghdad caliphate was the position of the caliph himself, above the government, above the law. He could and did concern himself with the higher things in life. He could and did overrule his vizier on matters of importance to him. He set aside special days on which he heard appeals and complaints from his subjects. So, although the caliphate was a political despotism, it was a one-man rule of a very special kind, which worked to the advantage of the arts and sciences.

In the eleventh century Baghdad's police were organized and efficient. The court system had progressed along with science and culture, and the people were protected from arbitrary rulings of petty officials by a Board for the Inspection of Grievances. There was a post office in every city and a relay arrangement like the much later American pony express to carry the mails. Pigeons were used to carry "air mail." The extensive roads were based on an old Persian system, with the highways emanating from Baghdad like spokes from a hub, reaching the far corners of the empire. Most famous of the four trunk roads, the Khurasan highway, stretched northeast through Hamadan, Rai, and Bukhara to Samarkand, and led to the border of China. Along this road and other great highways were connections with secondary roads leading to lesser cities, and a pilgrim could travel from China to the Red Sea without ever leaving the caliph's roads.

The decline of Abbasid power came in two ways: militarily and culturally.

The military decline began in the ninth century with the introduction by Caliph al-Mutawakkil of foreign units into the army. In the tenth century al-Muqtadir turned the defense of the provinces over to the governors, who paid their own troops and were responsible for them. The governors of the twenty-four provinces were chosen by the vizier, and as time went on, these offices tended to become hereditary, with each governor (emir) behaving like a king in his own realm.

Socially, the Abbasids began with the old Persian equality between men and women, but this broke down into slavery and concubinage. By the end of the tenth century women were segregated and confined to the harems. After three or four centuries most of the Persians in the caliphate were Muslimized.

Great change came to the caliphate in the matter of religion in the ninth century, with the birth of the Mu'tazilah movement. It started out as a liberal movement, which would encourage independent thought; the products of the human mind were regarded as superior to the word of the Koran. This theory held for a time, but in the tenth century Abu al-Hasan Ali al-Ash'ari of Baghdad founded "scholastic theology" in Islam, and his

theologians spent their lives trying to rationalize the
Koran with the modified Greek thought that the scientists
were devoloping. It was impossible from the beginning,
but Islam took it seriously.

Then, in 1058 a man was born who would fix the universal creed of Islam into a mold that would last a
thousand years. He was Abu Hamid al-Ghazzali, a native of the town of Kus in Khurasan. Al-Ghazzali studied
religion, philosophy, and science, he became an intellectual questioner, then underwent a profound emotional
experience and became a dervish, or holy man. He wrote
a book on the revival of the "science" of religion. He
made people take religion seriously again. Muslims either
loved or hated al-Ghazzali—there was no in-between.
Soon Islam was split badly by the difference in beliefs.
At the beginning of the tenth century the religious community of Qarmatians founded an independent state—
almost Communist in plan—on the western shore of the
Persian Gulf. They raided the pilgrim routes, and then
they seized Mecca and carried off the black stone
of the Kaaba. Next came another group called the Assassins—those fierce, mystical fanatics who gave the
English language a word for killer. At the end of the
eleventh century the Assassins terrorized the Muslim
world and even assassinated Vizier Nizam al-Mulik.

By this time the caliphate was in shreds. Spain, Morocco, Tunisia, and Egypt had all broken away. Al-
Saffar, the governor a major province, even threatened the caliphate in the tenth century. In the next century the descendants of Saman, a Zoroastrian noble of
Balkh, seized the province of Khurasan, established their
capital at Bukhara and a major city at Samarkand and

challenged Baghdad. One province after another came under the sway of its governor and paid either no fealty or only lip service to the rule of the caliphate.

In the ninth century the eighth Abbasid caliph, al-Mutasim, surrounded himself with a bodyguard of Turks from Transoxiana. Soon the generals were running the palace, and the caliph's rule hardly extended outside. Caliph murdered caliph or blinded him and sent him begging in the streets. (At one time three former caliphs lived in Baghdad, all blinded, all beggars.)

In 945 Caliph al-Mustakfi made a dictator of the powerful general Ahmad ibn-Buwayh. For the next century the descendants of ibn-Buwayh ruled the land, as much as it was ruled by anyone. By this time Baghdad had ceased to be the hub of the Muslim world, for scholarship and progress can hardly prosper in places of terror. Cultural leadership was moving to Shiraz, to Cairo, and to Cordova in Spain. And yet the Buwayhids made an attempt to consolidate the petty kingdoms and re-create the empire. They also patronized science and the arts, and built a great hospital in Baghdad, al-Bimaristan al-Adudi. There a staff of twenty-four physicians also served as faculty for a great medical school. The Buwayhids supported the sciences, built observatories, and commissioned translations of foreign works. But the trend was on the downgrade, even so.

By the middle of the eleventh century Shiites and Sunnite Muslims were quarreling everywhere. The governors had become petty kings and held their own kingdoms. Then came outright rebellion by the Seljuks, a clan of Turkomans from the Kirghiz steppes of Turkestan. They fought their way south, taking one territory after another until they came to the gates of Baghdad, where Caliph al-Qaam greeted the leader Tughril Beg as a deliverer, and made Tughril Beg sultan—that is, a lay ruler or king in place of the religious leader caliph. The former general of Baghdad, al-Bassasiri, took the capital again briefly, deposed Caliph al-Qaam, sent his emblems of power to Egypt. But the Seljuks came back and reinstated the caliph.

Then at the end of the twelfth century, the Mongols came. Genghis Khan's men stabled their horses in the mosques of Bukhara, killed 60,000 of the 100,000 people of Harat, and destroyed the beautiful cities of Samarkand, Balkh, and Khwarizm. By the opening of the thirteenth century the caliphs lived in a state of constant alarm lest the Mongols descend on them. Here was the beginning of the end.

In 1253 Hulagu, the grandson of Genghis Khan, left Mongolia with a vast army, and moved south. In the fall of 1257 Hulagu sent an ultimatum to Caliph al-Mustasim to destroy the Baghdad city wall and let the Mongols in. The caliph did not answer directly, and when the wall was breached, the angry Mongols plundered and burned the city so thoroughly that after a few days they had to withdraw, driven away by the stench of bodies in the streets. So the Mongol dynasty came to Baghdad, and Hulagu assumed the title Il-Khan. The Khans, his descendants, then turned their attention to cultural affairs and became converts to Islam, setting the stage for revival of some of the sciences. But it was never the same again in Baghdad.

8

The Scientific Change

THE second half of the eleventh century was the time of Omar Khayyám. Omar the poet was also the *only* great mathematician of the era. He devised cubic equations. He wrote love poems but he also studied physics. We know him for his poems. The sultan knew him for his mathematics. Omar's life and ideas also indicated the change in viewpoint of the caliphate. He divided the seekers of knowledge into four categories.

First in Omar's categories came the theologians. They, he said, were content with disputation and proofs from the Koran, considering this enough for anyone. Such persons believed a stone fell because God made it fall and not because of any innate properties of the stone or of some external force.

In Omar's second category were the philosophers and learned men of Greek inspiration who used rational arguments and sought to learn the laws of logic.

Third were the Ismailis, one branch of Shia Islam. The Shia sect came about basically as a family political dispute within Islam. The Shiites held that Ali and his successors were divinely ordained caliphs, that Husein of this family was a martyr. The sect became fanatic and bred the offshoots of Fatimite (followers of the Fatima line) and the Assassins. They and similar sects held that it was enough to accept information from "a learned and credible informant." In essence, then, they sought seers who cited the Koran.

Fourth were the Sufis, a variety of mystics who "sought knowledge" by attempting to cleanse their souls of impure thoughts. The soul was supposed to become so pure that the spiritual world and all truths would be reflected in it. Ignorance represented impurity of nature; if a man was pure enough, he would know everything there was to know.

Mysticism became the leading factor in eastern Muslim life in this period. Indeed, Omar Khayyám himself was a believer in Sufi mysticism. The group known as Illuminationists dominated Baghdad's thinking after the middle of the eleventh century. The Illuminationists accepted mysticism as a part of the universe. So although the materials of science were advanced by the Muslims until the middle of the eleventh century, when mysticism began to dominate, scientific thought declined.

Such decline, however, did not preclude certain advances in techniques and ideas, and this was true of the later period in the East.

The medical leader of the tenth century was the physician ibn-Jazla of Baghdad, who wrote a book describing 352 diseases and outlining courses of treatment for them. The book was called *Tables of the Bodies with Regard to Their Constitution*. Ismail al-Jurjani wrote a 450,000-word medical encyclopedia, the first to be done in Persian.

In the twelfth century, there were no important medical scientists in Baghdad. So much and so fast had things changed.

Libraries and observatories were still in existence, and still encouraged by the caliphs and their lesser nobles, so a certain body of astronomical and mathematical knowledge continued to be amassed. Indeed, in these later years the only scientific attainments of note in the eastern caliphate came in these fields.

One of Omar Khayyám's accomplishments is very little known, his famous calendar.

Under the caliphate, the Muslims had used for many years the old Persian calendar which divided the year into twelve months of thirty days each, and then added five days at the end to make up the solar year. The Sultan Maliksha Jalal al-Din ordered Omar to reform this calendar. His reformed calendar was more accurate than the Gregorian calendar in use in the West in the modern world; Omar's had only an error of one day in nearly four thousand years.

Except for Omar it was the age of the astronomers. Abu-l-Qasim Himatallah ibn-al-Hussain ibn Ahmad Badi al-Zaman was the greatest Muslim astronomer of the twelfth century. He lived in Isfahan and then Baghdad. He was in charge of astronomical observation at the palace of the sultan of Iraq, Mughith al-din Mahmud, and was known in Baghdad as al-Asturlabi, because he was the caliphate's most competent builder of astrolabes.

The most interesting mathematician and astronomer of the age was al-Khazini, a Greek slave who had acquired some education before he was enslaved. When his master learned that this slave had a grasp of scientific studies, he gave him an excellent scientific education in the schools at Marw. Al-Khazini then compiled a valuable set of astronomical tables, and later wrote a famous book on hydrostatics, mechanics, and physics. He went thoroughly into such subjects as specific gravity, giving tables for many liquids and solids. He discussed the theory of gravity, knowing that it was a force directed toward the center of the earth. He thought it a universal force and that the center of the earth was the center of the universe, but the facts of gravity and its effects did not elude him. He observed the gravity of air and measured the densities of liquids with instruments. He wrote the theory of the lever. He discussed the balance, as a means of leveling and of measuring time.

From time to time over the centuries, the various astronomers and astronomical teams had composed a *zij*. A zij was primarily a table of astronomical data, but included also theoretical discussions of astronomy and writings and diagrams of the mathematical astronomy involved. One such was the Ilkhanid Zij of the thirteenth century, one of the earliest to point out error in Ptolemaic astronomy. The Arab planetary system differed from Ptolemy's by putting the center of the earth at the center of the heavenly spheres, making earth center of the universe.

Just after the middle of the thirteenth century a brother of Hulagu Khan, a prince named Mangu, built two schools at Bukhara, each accommodating a thousand students. Mangu developed a strong interest in mathematics and astronomy, and it was said that he mastered part of Euclid without a teacher, and also that he planned the big observatory that was built at Pekin. Here was a new element in science—the beginning of contact between the science of Arabia and that of China through the Mongols.

Mangu's greatest work was an observatory at Maragheh in Azerbaijan. It was built on a hill outside the city, water was brought to it by water wheels, and it boasted a huge tower. The main building was domed, and the dome was holed and was used to measure the motion of the sun in degrees and minutes. The arrangement was such that the solar rays fell upon the threshold on the first day of spring. Inside the building there were celestial spheres, models of the epicycles (circular motions of the planets), illustrations of the phases of the moon and signs of the zodiac. There was a terrestrial globe made of paper pulp, and a celestial globe of metal, which later found its way to Dresden.

This expensive observatory was built for one basic purpose: to do the astronomical work necessary to carry out the astrological prophecies of the future demanded by Hulagu Khan. So his court astrologers had also to be astronomers, and very good ones.

The way of the scientist was never easy. Under the khans, a man's life was always on the line. It made no difference how important he had become, not even if he reached the very top.

Nasr al-Din al-Tusi was the great astronomer of the thirteenth century. He had taken service with Hulagu Khan before the march on Baghdad. When Baghdad fell, the khan called him and ordered a prediction as to whether the offensive would be successful. Nasr al-Din's enemies secretly suggested that if Hulagu killed the caliph, disaster would befall the Mongols. They knew he would kill the caliph. They knew Nasr al-Din did not dare suggest mercy. So Nasr al-Din predicted victory. He was right, and his reputation was made.

Later Hulagu ordered an official named Ala al-Din al-Juwayni put to death, and that officer's brother went to Nasr al-Din and asked him to save al-Juwayni. Nasr al-Din pointed out that once Hulagu had issued an order and publicized it, he never retracted.

Please, said the brother, save him.

There might be a way, said Nasr al-Din.

Nasr al-Din then set out toward Hulagu's court with a staff and astrolabe in hand, followed by a servant carrying a censer, incense, and fire.

When Nasr arrived at the gate, he kindled the incense and raised the astrolabe, as if making observations of the heavens. Hulagu's courtiers saw him and reported to the khan. After some time of "making observations," Nasr al-Din asked ostentatiously after the health of the khan. The courtiers said the great khan was well, whereupon Nasr al-Din threw himself on the ground and gave thanks to God for the good health of his sovereign. But several times, in the next hour, he asked after the health of the khan, as if he did not quite believe the courtiers.

Hulagu was in seclusion and had left orders that he would see no one. But when the khan heard that the great astrologer kept asking about his health, his curiosity was aroused, and he called for Nasr al-Din. What was happening, the khan asked, that caused Nasr al-Din to take so much interest in his health at the moment?

The astrologer put on his best face and told the khan that the ascendant planet of the day indicated an extremely dangerous situation for the khan. He, Nasr al-Din, was burning incense and making special prayers, asking God to turn calamity away from his ruler.

What could the khan do to facilitate this? the ruler asked.

Nasr al-Din suggested that Hulagu might send orders to all corners of the empire, freeing those in chains and forgiving those about to be executed. This mercy from the khan on earth should bring mercy from God in the heavens.

Hulagu sent out the message. Ala al-Din al-Juwayni was spared by Hulagu and Hulagu was spared by God. Nasr al-Din smiled secretly to himself.

Nasr al-Din was not a fraud. He was a scientist of his day, and if he was called upon to put his talents to work in fields other than science, he knew precisely what he was doing, and why. He always differentiated between his work of astronomy and that of astrology. One was science, the other was sorcery.

Nasr al-Din's power was soon so great that Hulagu would not take a trip unless the astrologer had advised him it was safe, and when Hulagu died, his son consulted Nasr al-Din before consenting to ascend the throne. Nasr had to make his horoscope then and there.

But Nasr's Ilkhani tables had nothing of mysticism about them, and Nasr was behind Hulagu's importation of a Chinese astronomer named Fao Mun-ji to Maragheh. Through Fao the Arabs learned much about Chinese astronomy and the Chinese calendar, while the Chinese took back with him to Peking the Ilkhani Tables.

The Maragheh Observatory was unique—first because it was very large and thus very expensive to maintain; second because it was the first Muslim observatory to outlive its founder. It functioned during the terms of seven different rulers, and lasted until after the beginning of the fourteenth century, when the dynasty fell. Then the observatory was soon nothing but ruins.

Intellectual activity shifted from Baghdad to Samar-

kand, and in the fifteenth century the grandson of Timur
(Tamerlane) the conqueror came to rule part of Khurasan and Mazandran, and then succeeded to the throne.
He was Ulugh Bey, a ruler with a great admiration for
astronomy and mathematics. He founded a very important observatory at Samarkand, and he himself was
the principal astronomer there. Under him were his
original teacher Qadizada, and two other astronomers.
He prepared very complete astronomical tables and a
star chart, and his astronomers carried out constant observations for thirty years here with the most modern
equipment available, including excellent water clocks.

In the sixteenth century the last great observatory in
eastern Araby was founded in Istanbul, under the Ottoman Turks. An astronomer named Taqi al-Din appealed
to the Sultan Murad, complaining that the astronomical
tables of the day were so far outdated that they did not
serve as good guides. The vizier was sympathetic and so
was the sultan, and so the observatory was built, but
immediately court intriguers turned Sultan Murad
against the observatory. During its building several important persons died suddenly. Then a plague struck the
empire. The mystics complained that the observers at
the observatory were interfering with the secrets of nature, and Sultan Murad heard and believed. The observatory was torn down. The impetus to scientific
achievement was dying in eastern Araby.

9

Egypt and Syria

WHILE science was riding high in the eastern regions, it was taking its own course in the middle of the Arab empire. At the close of the ninth century Shiites in Yemen began sowing seeds of unrest among the Muslims of Africa. Since Africa was a long way from Baghdad, they could espouse their outlawed beliefs openly there.

The result was that the Persian leader Said betook himself to North Africa, destroyed the Aghlabid family who had seized control there, and became the new ruler. He changed his name to Imam Ubaydullah al-Mahdi. Soon he extended his control over all of Morocco, Egypt, and Syria. By 973 his forces had moved to the Atlantic shore. This new empire called itself the Fatimid dynasty, for its descent through Fatima, the daughter of the Prophet. Cairo was the capital.

The Fatimid empire reached its zenith between 975 and 996, under the reign of Abu Mansur Nizar al-Aziz, when the empire stretched from the Atlantic to the Red Sea and included Mecca and Medina. Almost immediately the rot set in, for the Fatimids made the mistake of importing Turkish and Negro mercenary troops to replace their Arabs, but it would take some time in showing.

Meanwhile, in the second half of the ninth century, science and the arts took on an independent new life, in what might be called the middlewestern part of the Arab domain. In medicine, the first famous man was the Christian physician Yahya ibn-Sarafyun, known sometimes as Serapion the Elder. He was an expert on poisons and antidotes for poisons. He also knew a good deal about phlebotomy, or bleeding. In the tenth century, Ishaq al-Israili became physician to the Fatimid Caliph Ubaid Allah al-Mahdi, who suffered from bladder trouble. The middle Arabs were particularly interested in drugs and plants. One man, al-Tamimi made pharmaceutical experiments and wrote widely on materia medica, especially dealing with minerals and plants that might be used in treatment of disease. They had other specialties: the hygiene of pregnant women and of babies, and above all, ophthalmology, the study of diseases of the eyes. Manuscripts have been found that describe a successful operation for soft cataract by suction through a hollow tube. Indeed, the book, by ibn-Isa, became a standard work on the subject.

By the twelfth century, Fatimid science was flourishing, particularly in medicine. Doctors were exploring the work of Hippocrates and Galen, drugs, even sex and married life.

The most famous physician of this time and place, and a very important figure in all of Arab letters, was the Jewish physician ibn-Maymun, known in the West as Maimonides. He was born in Cordova and studied there, but he moved to Cairo in 1165 as a result of persecution of the Jews. In Cairo he became court physician to the sultan of Egypt and Syria, Saliah al-din, known to the

Third Crusaders as Saladin, and to his son al-Malik al-Aziz. Maimonides' medical practice was based on Galen, as transmitted by Rhazes, but he improved many methods of treatment himself. He found a new method of circumcision, he treated hemorrhoids successfully, and his work *On Health* became a standard text on hygiene in its time and for two hundred years thereafter. He was most notable for his independence of mind, at a time when Islamic science tended to become encyclopedic rather than experimental.

The most popular of Maimonides' medical writings was his *Medical Principles,* a collection of 1,500 aphorisms and critical remarks about anatomy, physiology, pathology, diagnosis and symptoms, aetiology (the cause of disease), treatments, fevers, bloodletting and cathartics and emetics, surgery, gynecology, hygiene, gymnastics and massage as treatment, bathing, dietetics, and drugs. This vast work gave a very good understanding of the *total* practice of medicine in the Arab world.

Once when Saladin's eldest son was very ill, Maimonides wrote an explanation of the case, gave the court general dietetic and hygienic rules to follow, wrote down remedies, and gave other instruction in the case to cure the patient.

Troubles of the eye had always been a serious problem in this section of the Arab empire, and much time was spent studying them. For a long time this Syro-Egyptian kingdom led the world in this aspect of medical science. A good and useful eye hospital was built in Cairo in the thirteenth century, then expanded to treat all disease. It had special wards for segregating various diseases: ophthalmia, dysentery, and malaria. The doctors even treated mental illness here, so far advanced were they. The hospital had laboratories, a dispensary, a kitchen, and many baths, and the doctors taught students in special lecture rooms.

At the end of the twelfth century came several significant Arabic works on ophthalmology, one by a Cairo oculist, abu-al-Fadail ibn-al-Naqud, another by Khalifah of Aleppo, who was skilled at eye surgery, particularly the removal of cataracts.

During the Fatimid period, one of the most important contributions to general learning was the erection of the Dar al-Hikmah, the Hall of Wisdom, which was established primarily for the teaching of the Shiite Muslim belief, but soon developed into a much broader institution, and astronomy and medicine were taught there.

Astronomy prospered here, too, for the usual reason. The Fatimid Caliph Al-Hakim was interested in astrology. Thus al-Hakim's court boasted two of the most prominent astronomers in the history of the Arabic sciences. One was ibn-Yunus, and the other was ibn-al-Haitham, better known as Alhazen.

Ibn-Yunus was born sometime around the middle of the tenth century and, after studying the sciences, became one of Islam's most prominent astronomers. He prepared new astronomical tables after making many observations himself and using those of others made at Cairo in the House of Wisdom. These observations were part of a plan set in motion by the Fatimid Caliph al-Aziz, and they were completed in the reign of al-Hakim. The astronomers watched eclipses and conjunctions of planets, they improved their knowledge of astronomical constants, such as the ecliptic and the apogee of the sun.

(The ecliptic is the apparent path of the sun across the heavens, and the apogee is the point in the orbit of a celestial body at which it is farthest from its center.) Ibn-Yunus also used trigonometry extensively in solving astronomical problems.

Alhazen was known as much for his work in physics as for astronomy and mathematics, for he was Islam's finest physicist and one of the world's most apt students of optics. His name was really Abu Ali al-Hasan ibn-al-Hasan ibn-al-Haitham. He was born in al-Basrah around 965, and then he moved to Egypt, where he became an important figure in the court of al-Hakim.

Alhazen's work in optics changed the world. His greatest book was *Optics (Kitab al-Mansir).* Here he improved on the knowledge of optical reflection inherited from the science of Greece. He also made a long investigation of the phenomenon of refraction of light, and he went into the laws of reflection of light as well. The Greeks had studied reflection in terms of plane mirrors. Alhazen used concave and parabolic mirrors, and learned to make his own mirrors. He discovered spherical aberration—the distortion of lenses. He established mathematically an exact focus for a paraboloid. One reason for his greatness was his ability to combine synthesis, experimentation, and analysis in addressing a problem, which meant simply that he took knowledge from many sources, fitted it together as a puzzle, found missing pieces by experiment, and then was able to stand off and measure what he had found in terms of its effects and importance.

Alhazen was the first to use the camera obscura. This was a lightproof box, with a lens. The rays of light entered the lens and formed an image on the opposite surface; it differed from a modern photographic camera in that the image was not recorded permanently. He studied the phenomenon of twilight, noting that it comes on when the sun is 19 degrees below the horizon. He also showed that when a person looks at an object, it is the object that is the source of light, and not the eye, as Euclid and Ptolemy had believed.

This Muslim discovered a basic theory of refraction of light: that transparency eases and quickens light while increased density slows it. It was many years before Europeans "proved" his studies by their own experiments. Oddly enough, even so great a genius as Sir Isaac Newton, hundreds of years later, was wrong about the nature of refraction, while Alhazen was correct. Newton's investigations were more profound and the results were obviously more effective on science and society, yet it is interesting to realize that in the eleventh century Alhazen understood the course of a ray of light. He understood that light takes the easier and quicker way to any point. Most important, he was a good experimenter, at a time when few others realized the importance of controlled experiment.

As was so often the case, Alhazen discovered that laboring under the eye of a caliph presented its problems. At one time he was assigned to find a formula for regulating the overflow of the Nile River. He failed, and fearful of al-Hakim's anger, he pretended that he had gone mad and hid from the caliph's sight until al-Hakim died. Perhaps that gave Alhazen time—at least somewhere he found the time to write a hundred different works on mathematics, astronomy, physics, philosophy, and medicine.

Cairo's scientific progress was spotty. In 1068 the city was looted by Turks, who carried off half the 200,000 volumes in the royal library, burning the books for their campfires and using the bindings as leather for their saddles and bridles.

And the Europeans did not help much. Part of the reason for the decline of science in Egypt was the Crusades, and all the difficulty they brought to the Middle East at the close of the eleventh century. They fought back and forth for years, and as they fought, the men of science moved elsewhere.

10

The Arabs of
the West

THE THIRD great Arab empire of the Middle Ages was located in Spain, and it is the one that most profoundly affected Western history.

By the middle of the eighth century, the empire established by the Arabs had been extended to the Pyrenees Mountains of Europe and was prospering in Spain. The Arabs would go no farther.

Spain was then a part of the Umayyad empire; the Abbasids had not yet rebelled.

When the Abbasids massacred the Umayyads, the two grandsons of Hisham (the tenth caliph of Damascus) escaped the slaughter and sought refuge in a Bedouin camp on the east bank of the Euphrates River. Suddenly, the black flags of the Abbasid searching party appeared near the camp, and the two boys fled into the river, to swim across. Abbasid followers stood on the east bank and promised the boys that, if they would come back, nothing would happen to them. The younger boy, thirteen, believed them and turned back. He was slain. The older, twenty, did not believe and swam across the river to safety.

This boy was Abd al-Rahman ibn-Muawiyah, the heir to the Umayyad caliphate.

This youth who had been raised in luxury suddenly

found himself quite alone, penniless, and with thousands of enemies in the world. Indeed, where did he have friends?

There was only one place, and that was Spain, more than halfway across the empire. He found help in Palestine, in the form of a faithful servant, Badr. He was nearly assassinated in North Africa. He and Badr wandered west for five years, penniless, until they reached Ceuta at the Strait of Gibraltar. He then sent Badr across to Spain, and that servant secured the loyalty of the Syrian soldiers who were stationed there. A ship was sent, Abd al-Rahman boarded it and crossed. Soon he was marching through the countryside, welcomed by the Umayyad soldiers who dominated this area. Yusuf ibn-Abd al-Rahman al-Fihri, the Abbasid governor, challenged Abd al-Rahman on the banks of the Guadalquivir River. Abd al-Rahman's forces won, he moved on to capture Cordova and declared a general amnesty, while Yusuf fled north.

For the next few years the redheaded Abd al-Rahman consolidated his empire. Abbasid Caliph al-Mansur sent a new governor to Spain. Abd al-Rahman sent back his head, preserved in camphor and salt. In 777 a group of Arab chiefs in the north invited Charlemagne to march into Spain, and he came as far as Saragossa in 778, but was stopped there and had to retreat. It was on this retreat that the Frankish rear guard was wiped out at Roncesvalles, Spain, August 14, 778—a defeat that gave rise to the romantic legend of Roland.

Abd al-Rahman began to create a new culture in Spain. He built buildings, palaces, mosques, libraries, aqueducts, and gardens. He built bridges and roads, and

he established the climate of intellectual growth. Under
his emirate, or governorship, Christians and Jews began
to flock to Spain. Some became Muslims, and they were
more privileged than the others. A Christian or a Jew
could rise high if he had something to offer, but it was
better to be a Muslim, even if the *muwalladun* (adopted
ones) were looked down upon by the Muslim Arabs.
Yet as time went on, the muwalladun became the ma-
jority of the populations of several centers.

In the next hundred years, all Islam was shaken by
uprisings and struggles for power, but Cordova remained
serene, and here there was intellectual progress. The
stage was set for development that was much like that of
the eastern regions, partly beholden to them, and yet
not quite the same.

First, Spain inherited from eastern Araby its slightly
earlier development of a high stage of culture and scientific attainment. In the eastern regions, the traditions
of Greece and Rome had already been combined with
those of India, and this amalgamated culture had been
carried to Spain.

Second, Spain benefited from the unity of Islam.
Wherever the Muslim religion went, the language, customs, and beliefs of the people were the same, and they
had common roots and shared many associations. Thus
the advances in knowledge and thought of the eastern
regions were readily available to Muslim leaders in
Spain.

Third, Spain's vast mixture of peoples, cultures, and
languages stimulated intellectual activity and gave Arab
leaders closer contact with European culture.

By the time of Abd al-Rahman II (821–852), Cordova had become a scholarly center that any nation could claim with pride. During the rule of his grandson, Abd al-Rahman III (912–961), the capital was famed far and wide for its power and brilliance. The first ruler in Spain to proclaim himself caliph, al-Rahman III was noted as a protector of culture and science. His successor, al-Hakam II, was himself a student of the arts and sciences. He sent his agents into every part of Islam to buy manuscripts, and he collected a library that amounted to 400,000 volumes, with a catalogue that filled forty-four volumes by itself.

In this al-Hakam was assisted by Hasday ben Shaprut, also known as Aub Yusuf, a famous Jewish physician born after 900, whom historian Aldo Mieli credits with transferring the center of intellectual Judaism from Iraq to Spain.

After al-Hakam came the long, relatively peaceful reign of the Caliph al-Hisam, which was very favorable for the development of the sciences. As it was in eastern Araby, even after the caliphate at Cordova fell, science and art continued to flourish for a time. Because of the nearness to Europe—that mingling of languages beneath the veneer of Arabic and that contact of the western Arabs with Europeans—there came a transmission of the culture of Islam to the West. It might not have been possible under any other circumstances.

At the height of its glory, the Spanish Umayyad capital of Cordova was one of three cultural centers of the world. (The other two were Constantinople and Baghdad.) Cordova had a population of 500,000 people, who lived in 113,000 houses. It had twenty-one suburbs, seventy libraries, and uncounted bookshops. There were

many miles of paved streets lighted by lamps, and at a
time when people in northern Europe sloshed through
mud and seldom took baths, the three hundred public
baths of Cordova provided a place of meeting and amusement as well as hygiene.

Spain was a wealthy land. It was the home of a leather
industry that was envied throughout Europe, and the
capital housed 13,000 weavers, who worked with silk
and wool. Other centers in the kingdom produced glass-
ware, brass, pottery, and steel. Toledo was famous for
its swords and daggers, for the art of inlaying steel with
gold and silver had been brought there from Damascus.
The Spanish Arabs were apt students of agriculture, too.
They dug canals and planted. They introduced a dozen
new products to Europe: rice, apricots, peaches, oranges,
cotton, saffon, and others.

Cultural contact with eastern Islam was made easier
by a lively trade with Baghdad and even Mecca. At this
time the Arabs ruled the seas. The Mediterranean and
the Red Sea were both Muslim lakes, and Arab ships
and boats navigated the deep waters of the Indian Ocean,
sailing to India and beyond to trade.

With such munificence the cultural level of Spain rose
rapidly. Soon there were nearly thirty free schools in
the capital, and the principal mosque was also a great
university, deemed better in its time than the mosque al-
Azhar of Cairo or the mosque Nizamiya of Baghdad.
Muslims, Christians, and others came from all parts of
Araby, from Europe and Asia to study here. All this
occurred at a time when only a handful of northern
Europeans could read and write, and these Europeans
were almost uniformly confined to the monasteries.

During the reign of Hisham II, the western Arab nation was actually ruled by Muhammad ibn-abi Amir, who rose to be royal chamberlain and vizier. He strengthened the kingdom and extended its boundaries, taking the name al-Mansur bi Allah ("Made Victorious Through the Aid of Allah"). Six years after al-Mansur's death, the kingdom began to fall apart. Hisham was forced to abdicate, and then one caliph followed another, each murdering or otherwise doing away with his predecessor, until the nobles and soldiers rose up in 1027 and abolished the caliphate altogether. Spain then crumbled into a number of petty states that fought endlessly among themselves.

But while it flourished, Arab science in Spain was as glorious as it ever had been in Baghdad.

It took some time after the establishment of the proper conditions for learning before many figures arose who were capable of important original work. In the court at Cordova, the first of these was Hasday ben Shaprut, the Jewish physician to Abd al-Rahman III.

One day the sultan received a Greek manuscript of Dioscorides' *De Materia Medica* from the emperor of Byzantium. Cordova did not have a Greek heritage the way that Baghdad did. Knowing this, the emperor sent along a Greek-speaking monk named Nicholas, who began working with Hasday and other Arabic-speaking physicians to put names of the plants and drugs into Arabic. Thus was established a tradition for Spanish Arab medicine.

The great writer on surgery in the Spanish Arab world was Abu-al-Qasim, known in the West as Albucasis. He was born in the middle of the tenth century and died

about 1013, after serving as court physician to al-Hakam
II, who ruled between 961 and 976. Albucasis was most
famous for his medical encyclopedia, *Al-Tasrif*, a work
that comprised thirty sections. It dealt with the preparation of drugs, sometimes by distillation, but its most
useful part was that dealing with surgery. Much of this
work came down from Paul of Aegina, the last represen-
tative Greek medical writer before the Muslim rise. But
Albucasis did not confine himself to parroting the information in the seven books of Paul; he added his own
observations and remarks. One very valuable part of
the book was the use of drawings of the surgical instruments of the period, with detailed accounts of surgical
procedures.

Albucasis told why surgery had not made much
progress among the Arabs. Largely, he said, it was because the Arab students were not adequately informed
about Galen and the other Greek and Roman practitioners. Also it was because theology prevented them
from practicing dissection openly (although a number
of surgeons did so secretly). The difficulty of perfecting
surgery without actual observation and knowledge secured through dissection did remain a major deterrent
to surgical progress under the Arabs.

The surgical discussions of Albucasis included works
on cautery, which he recommended in many cases, including apoplexy, epilepsy, and dislocations of joints.
One book dealt with surgical operations. He advised all
who would practice surgery first to know precisely the
disease they were treating, and then to make sure that
they knew what they were doing before picking up the
knife. (A surgeon must never operate simply for the sake

of operating, or for profit, because almighty God was always looking over his shoulder.) Albucasis described several methods of surgical treatment. One was lithotomy, cutting into the bladder. Another was treatment of hernia by cutting. He told how to treat abdominal wounds. He suggested that in the case of intestinal injuries, the edges of tissue be placed together and then that large ants be applied. The ants locked their jaws into the tissue, providing a sort of safety-pin suture. (The system is still used in parts of Africa.)

Albucasis also described the other usual surgical procedures of his day, trephining (opening the skull), amputation, and operations for goiter and other externally observable disorders. Human teeth could be replaced; he recommended that beef bone be used. He described catheters and catheterization, and methods and forms of suture. He wrote a good deal on fractures and dislocations. He also wrote on styptics and obstetrics and treatment by surgery of difficulties in the eyes and ears.

Oddly enough, the knowledge and practices of Albucasis received relatively little attention in his day among Muslims, because the religious and cultural prejudices against surgery grew rather than decreased. The importance of Albucasis would not truly be felt until his work was handed along to the Christians of Europe, and then for a long time he would be regarded as one of the leading figures in his field.

The first half of the twelfth century produced several remarkable clinicians and thoughtful students of the practice and philosophy of medicine. At least two of them were members of the same family, the ibn-Zuhr. First of these was abu-l-Ala-Zuhr ibn-Abu Marwan Abd al-

Malik ibn-Muhammad ibn-Marwan al-Ishbili, known more commonly as Abu-l-Ala Zuhr. He was the son of a medical family of Arabs who lived in eastern Andalusia from the beginning of the tenth century until the Christians drove them out in the middle of the thirteenth century. His father, Abu Marwan Abd al-Malik, had left the family hearth in the eleventh century to practice in Cairo, which he did with great success for a number of years as diagnostician, then came home to retire.

Abu-l-Ala studied at Cordova and became a very successful physician himself. He joined the court of al-Mutamid, ruler of Seville, between 1068 and 1091, and when that court was overthrown by the Berbers, Abu-l-Ala became an official under the conqueror, Yusuf ibn-Tashfin.

Abu-l-Ala's son was the greatest doctor in the world, in his time. He was called Abu Marwan ibn-Zuhr (although his full name was even longer and more complicated than his father's). His fame moved to the Christian world even in his lifetime, and there he was known as Avenzoar.

Born in Seville in the early years of the 1090's, Avenzoar studied with his father and other physicians, and traveled in Africa for a time, then he returned to Seville, where he became vizier and physician to Abd al-Mumin, founder of the Muwahhid dynasty there.

This physician wrote six important medical books. The three that remain established his position as leading medical man of his time. One book was called *The Book of the Iqtisad*. It is a summary of methods of treatment and hygiene for the benefit of lay readers. Second was a work called *Kitab Al-Taisir Fi-l-Mudawat Wal Tadbir,* or *The Book, Simplifying Therapeutics and Diet.* It describes many conditions of illness, and the treatment of them, and also gives a list of drugs and their uses. Avenzoar's third book was another study of the use of drugs and hygiene.

Avenzoar had many of the attributes of his time, some of which were not very helpful to the progress of medical science. He looked upon the practice of surgery as beneath the dignity of a physician. He, in fact, would not even prepare his own medicines. He was not unique in this attitude, but his espousal of the negative position did much to strengthen it, since he became so important to the Western world later on. The attitude of Avenzoar in this regard was one of the most harmful of all to medicine, for it led to difference and struggle between physicians and surgeons that lasted for hundreds of years.

Nonetheless, Avenzoar presented positive and useful attitudes and information for his successors. He treated tumors, heart disease, intestinal disease, and paralysis. He spoke of treating the inflammation of the middle ear, and described skin diseases. He understood physiology well enough to recommend artificial feeding when necessary, and he discussed the need for tracheotomy to avoid choking.

Avenzoar lived until 1161 at Seville, an honored and respected noble of the court, and then he was followed by one son, Abu Bakr Muhammad ibn-Abd al-Malikibn Muhammad ibn Marwan al-Ishbili, often called al-Hafid, or "the grandson," who was born in Seville around 1110, and also became a physician, as well as a poet and literary figure. Al-Hafid wrote an important treatise on eye disease. Late in life al-Hafid became involved in

political matters, and he was poisoned in Marrakesh in
1199.

A younger contemporary of Avenzoar, whose life and
work moved into the last half of the century, was Abu-l-
Walidy Muhammad ibn-Ahmad ibn-Muhammad ibn-
Rushd, known also as Averroes. He cooperated with
Avenzoar in one medical-philosophical study, Avenzoar
writing his book on therapeutics and diet as a companion
piece to Averroes' more philosophical study of life call
Al Kulliyat, or *Generalities of Medicine.*
Averroes belonged to a wealthy and important family
in Cordova. Averroes prepared for law and medicine
at the university in the mosque at Cordova. Later, he
went to Marrakesh to study. Unlike Avenzoar, Averroes
was a man of many interests, and one of these was jurisprudence. His father and grandfather had each been
qadi of Cordova, or judge in this theological society.
Averroes became qadi of Seville, and then of Cordova.
Marrakesh, in Africa, had by this time become the political center of the region, and the caliph there, Abu Yaqub
Yusuf, called Averroes to Marrakesh to become his physician. He also served the succeeding caliph Yaqub al-
Mansur, but the second caliph became displeased, as so
often happened, and banished Averroes to Lucena, a
town near Cordova, ordering that all his books (except
the strictly scientific ones) be burned. Near the end of
the twelfth century, he was restored to favor and returned to Marrakesh to die.

Al Kulliyat was Averroes' great medical work. In
seven books he dealt with anatomy, physiology, pathology, diagnosis, materia medica (the drugs and other
substances used in the concoction of healing remedies),

hygiene, and general medical practice, among other things. He was the first to note, for example, that no one caught smallpox twice.

As time went on, Averroes turned more to the study of philosophy. (He wrote the *Kulliyat* before 1162, and thereafter most of his writing concerned philosophy, logic, and ethics, although he did write a commentary on Galen's *De febribus* in 1193.) He engaged in a philosophical dispute with al-Ghazzali, holding generally to the peripatetic views of Aristotle, as opposed to al-Ghazzali's mysticism, and this dispute was the cause of Averroes' disgrace.

Averroism held that the whole world, all at once, is created by God, directly, eternally, and continuously. His European followers held that the system was fully determined, it was organic, and it was evolutionary, permeated by a single power (God.) This philosophy exerted considerable influence in the emerging culture of Europe a few years later.

The first half of the eleventh century turned out to be the climactic period of Arab thought and intellectual activity. In this period the slight lag of western Islam was made up. The books of eastern Araby were moving freely across the Mediterranean, and the philosophers and scientists of Cordova and the other cities of Spain were doing some of history's great work.

In this period the mathematician al-Karmani seems to have introduced the writings of the mystical Brethren of Purity into Spain.

It was given to the last half of the century to produce much original mathematical and astronomical work in the western part of Islam. Al-Zarqali, known to the west as Arzachel, was the most talented observer of his time (1029–1087). He not only studied the astrolabe and its uses, he improved on it and invented a better one, which the Muslims called the *safiha*. He wrote about solar apogees in relation to the stars, and he was the first to prove that the sun did "move" relative to the earth, that there was a seasonal change in the appearances.

Then came a figure known as Jabir ibn-Aflah, who was sometimes also known as Geber to the Latin-speaking Europeans in Spain. This fact, plus the fact that others were writing various treatises on many subjects and using the Geber name, lent to the confusion that has grown up surrounding the Geber (Jabir ibn-Haiyon) of the eighth century in the eastern caliphate. But Jabir ibn-Aflah was an astronomer and mathematician who lived much of his life in Seville. His importance to science is his criticism of the theories of Ptolemaic astronomy.

In the second half of the twelfth century lived Abu Ishaq al-Bitruji al-Ishbili Nur al-din, or al-Bitruji for short, another Muslim astronomer. He has come down in Latin as Alpetragius. He and his work marked the climax of a rebellion in Muslim astronomy against the cosmology of Ptolemy. The astronomical observers noticed that their most careful observations did not agree with the astronomical almanacs and the ephemerides, or tables that supposedly gave the position of every heavenly body of every day of the year. As the ephemerides continued to move further away from the observed facts, it was apparent that something was wrong with the tables. But instead of looking for new answers, al-Bitruji and his associates proposed to return to an earlier Greek theory, that of homocentric spheres. (No one in the world in this period ever conceived of the idea that the movements of heavenly bodies could be elliptical, the sphere was regarded as perfect, and the Arabs were unable to transcend this "perfection.") This was the old Eudoxian theory, developed in the fourth century B.C. Eudoxus theorized that there were twenty-seven different spheres, accounting thus for the movement of the sun, moon, planets, and stars, all of them—said the theory —revolving around the earth. Aristotle had accepted the principle, but used fifty-five spheres in his explanation of the heavenly movements.

The theory of al-Bitruji was called the theory of spiral motion. It was quite complex, involving nine spheres, with a heavenly body attached to each of the first eight spheres and a ninth sphere, outside that of the fixed stars, given motive power, and called the "prime mover." The prime mover caused each of the other spheres to move from east to west, speed depending on the distance of each sphere from the prime mover. The fixed stars and their sphere, for example, were said to move one revolution in twenty-four hours, being closest to the prime mover. The moon, which was farthest away, took twenty-five hours. The various bodies had their own motions. It was a very complicated system. It was hailed in its time as a "new astronomy" and much was made of it in the Arab world.

11

Other Sciences
in Western Islam

AMONG the intellectual studies taken up by the Muslims of Spain during the second half of the tenth century was history. Ibn al-Qutiya wrote of Andalusia from the time of the Muslim conquest until the end of the ninth century, and a work on the conjugation of Arabic verbs. Much more important, at the same time several Jewish students were working on aspects of Hebrew and Arabic that would tend to assist the free flow of scientific language in the future. Thus were formed the tools that would make it possible for talented and industrious Jewish scientists and translators to work with the two Semitic languages, Hebrew and Arabic.

The first half of the eleventh century was marked everywhere in the Muslim world by the development of philosophy and a new concern for the ways of the world. In Spain one important figure was the Jewish philosopher ibn-Gabirol, sometimes known as Yahya ibn-Jabirul, or to the West as Avicebron, bringer of the philosophy of Neoplatonism to the notice of Europe.

New in this period several factors were arising to educate western Europe to the fact that an advanced science and civilization did exist among the Arabs and the lands they had conquered. The Crusaders going east were impressed with the opulence of Muslim society, and some thinking ones brought home stories of the attainments of that society as well. The Christian monk Gerbert, who was born in Spain fairly early in the tenth century, studied in Barcelona for a time, and although this was then Christian territory, it had a strong Muslim flavor and Arabic influence was felt there. Gerbert, it is known, was familiar with the Hindu-Arabic numeral system, for example, and he went on to become Pope Sylvester II, and carried to Rome itself some knowledge of this superior civilization.

A third factor in this surge was the establishment of a church school at Salerno, just south of the Bay of Naples. As early as the ninth century physicians at Salerno had a fair knowledge of Greek medicine, a heritage from the glorious past when Salernum had been a Roman health resort. In the interim, the place had been attacked and pillaged by the Arabs, so the people of Salerno were familiar with the forces to the south and east of them. Here arose the first medical school in Europe, without much Arabic influence at first, but that would come.

In the 1000's the Muslims of Spain were taking an interest in many fields of science. Al-Hakri of Cordova wrote a geography of the region, *Book of Roads and the Provinces,* which was lost. He also wrote a geographical dictionary and a book on the principal plants and trees of Andalusia.

In the second half of the eleventh century, language problems become less important. Earlier they had barred the passage of Arabic thought to Europe. The first major break came with the work of Constantinus Africanus, or Afer, who was born in Carthage and grew up

in Araby. Afer traveled widely throughout the eastern
world. He worked at Antioch for a time. Then he came
to Europe. For a while he lived at Salerno, and there
he told the monks and students of the civilization of the
east by translating from Arabic to Latin; because he was
very knowledgeable about the scientific achievements of
the Muslims, he began opening eyes. He translated parts
of Galen (whose works had now gone from Greek to
Arabic to Latin). He translated Albucasis and Rhazes.
He remained at Salerno long enough to show the priests
and doctors the wonders that existed in another world,
and then he went on to Monte Cassino in Italy, to
spread the word farther, much farther.

Meanwhile Muslim men of science were assessing
the progress of the sciences, even as western Europe
was eagerly beginning to learn of the works of the scientists of the past.

The great geographer of Muslim Spain was Abu Ab-
dallah Muhammad ibn-Muhammad ibn-Abd allah ibn-
Idris. He was a descendant of Mohammad the Prophet
through his daughter Fatima and was interesting because
the career of al-Idrisi, as he was called, marked a sharp
departure in the history of Islamic science. Al-Idrisi was
born in Ceuta around 1100, and he studied in the usual
Muslim pattern in the schools and mosque universities
of Spain, most illustriously at Cordova, but his major
work was done in the Christian courts of Sicily.

Sicily had been a Byzantine stronghold until the ninth
century, when it was captured by the Arabs, who established the Aghlabid dynasty. The Arabs dominated
the culture and the language for two hundred years. Then
Count Roger and his Normans took the island. Roger I,

as he was called then, established a government that looked kindly upon the fruits of Arab civilization. The king had no formal education, but he had the common sense to understand the need for it and to respect what his former enemies had accomplished. He encouraged the growth of a Christian-Islamic culture that permitted the Christians to begin picking the flowers of Muslim science. He patronized Arab scholars and allowed the Muslims freedom of religion and their own social ways. In fact, the government became a mixture of Norman and Muslim, with several Muslims holding the highest positions in the land.

Roger I's son, Roger II, dressed like a Muslim, even to a robe that was decorated in Arabic characters. He gave commissions to Muslim architects, who built the cities in Muslim style, employed Muslim soldiers, and his fleet, the greatest in the Mediterranean, was commanded by a Greek who had formerly been in the service of a Muslim prince.

Al-Idrisi came to this court, attracted by the freedom and friendliness of the Norman rulers. The masterwork he produced at this sunny court was a book of geography called *The Recreation for Him Who Yearns to Travel.* This book was the finest description of the physical world ever prepared in medieval times, for it described in detail both Christian countries and Muslim countries, the peoples and the lands. It summed up the geographical studies of Ptolemy and al-Masudi, and corrected many old errors, basing its information on actual reports of travelers who were sent out from Sicily by the king to bring back the information wanted. Al-Idrisi showed his complete familiarity with the spherical na-

ture of the earth here and by building a silver planisphere, a globe of the heavens, and a dish-shaped map of
the world.

So well entrenched was al-Idrisi at this court that
after Roger II's death, he continued in Palermo under
the rule of William I, writing another geography.

One can see how the Muslims spread out across the
world, given the power of their rule and their curiosity
for learning. Abu-l-Hussain Muhammed ibn-Ahmad al-
Kinani, known as ibn-Jubair, left Valencia in the twelfth
century, studied at nearby Jativa, went to Mecca and
the Near East, and seemed to spend most of his life
traveling in the Arab empire and making notes. He was
an indefatigable recorder of fact. He noted the types and
natures of the ships on which he traveled across the
Mediterranean. He described hospitals and the geography
of the regions through which he passed. He left an excellent description of life in Sicily under William II.

Muslims made other studies in the West. Abu Zakariya
Yahy ibn-Muhammed ibn-Ahmad ibn-al-Awwam al-
Ishbili was an agriculturist who lived at Seville in the
last days of the twelfth century. His *Kitab al-Falaha
(Book of the Farmer)* is the most important medieval
work in any language on agriculture. It was based on
Greek and other Arabic studies, but it also continued
the fruits of Spanish Arab experience with cattle raising,
poultry farming, the bee culture, the raising of some
585 different plants and more than fifty kinds of fruit
trees. The author was familiar with differences in soils
and the properties of manure. He discussed grafting and
even the diseases of plants.

Yet in the twelfth century the trend was away from

original work to encyclopedia writing. The bloom was off the rose, at least as regards the advancement of individual efforts in science. In a way it was the same as with the eastern regions, the complications of philosophy and theology and the fragmentation of Muslim power everywhere had a definite effect on the sciences. The decline began in the second half of that golden age of the eleventh century, even as contemporaries must have believed their society was achieving ever new gains.

Considering science as international and not as Muslim or Greek or Western, the twelfth century represented a breathing space and a period of transmission. In the ninth, tenth, and eleventh centuries, the Arabs and other Arabic-speaking people had obtained the basis for their achievements by an infusion of translations. Now they would be translated in turn.

Yet Islam continued to make advances in science, particularly in the astronomical sciences, for centuries to come. The period we know as the golden age of Arabic science ended in eastern Araby with the capture of Hulagu of Baghdad in 1258, and in western Araby with the seizure of Cordova, the capital of Muslim thought, by the Christian king, Ferdinand III, in 1236.

Nonetheless, the torch was passed to the West beginning in the twelfth century, and the Westerners felt the same thrills and enthusiasms, that Arab discoverers had known in the seventh, as they, too, began soaking up the wealth of wisdom that had come from Greece and Rome, India and Persia, and very much from the Islamic Fertile Crescent as well.

12

The Sum of Arab Science

BETWEEN the seventh and thirteenth centuries there was no society other than the Arab that was capable of supporting scientific inquiry. But in all three kingdoms of Islam, what did the Arabs really do for science in the seven hundred years they were in power? The Arabic-speaking people saved many works of the ancient Mediterranean world, snatched them from the burning as it were, and then passed them along virtually without change. Is this all the Arabs did?

There was much more.

In the field of medicine, for example, the Arabs invented the science of pharmacy. True, the example is a little ragged, for the most authoritative writer in the field of materia medica, Iban al-Baitar, lived in the first half of the thirteenth century. He came from Malaga, traveled the eastern regions of the empire, and then became physician to the Egyptian emirs and taught in the medical school at Cairo. He added up the works of Dioscorides and Galen and the previous Arabic writers in the field, and produced a *Corpus of Simples,* which even in the twentieth century was respected by scientists. It included 1,400 drugs, some three hundred of them introduced for the first time. At the same time in Cairo al-Kuhin al-Attaar al-Israili wrote the best text that had yet appeared in the world on the subject of pharmacy, giving professional standards for pharmacists and directions for the gathering of drug plants and substances, known as simples, and the preparation of drugs from these. Yet beginning with the tenth century, too, Arab and Persian pharmacists began shipping their drugs to Europe.

In the practice of medicine, Arabic-speaking physicians made considerable strides forward. Surgery did not fare so well, given the prohibitions of religious law against practical study of anatomy, but the practice of medicine was extended, so was the teaching of it, and in the field of ophthalmology great strides were made. Clinical observation was improved, and so was the knowledge of practical medical chemistry. The Arab studies of plants and animals were unsystematic, in a botanical sense, if useful in a medical sense. They advanced the science of toxicology from alchemical tracts to rational medicine, and the Arabs Rhazes and Avicenna were the forerunners of modern psychotherapy. They and other doctors were also extremely competent in the field of diet. They set up the first great hospitals, in which they treated patients, taught physicians by practice in the hospitals, and carried out scientific research.

The concept of exact science was given a new meaning by the Arabs. Al-Farabi and others came very close to the establishment of experimental laboratory science. Rhazes reached the conclusion that there is an intelligible order in the world and that man can grasp that order and use it for his own ends—a new concept. Science in the time of the ancients tended toward metaphysical speculation, and much of it was bound up in mysteries.

The Arabs venerated the Greeks and other ancients, but not so much that they did not attempt to verify all the facts given them. They went far toward developing an objective attitude that we regard in the modern world as "scientific."

In mathematics the Arabs released many of the strictures on thought by the introduction of the Hindu-Arabic numeral system and the development of practical rules of arithmetic. They invented algebra, which made it possible for them to manipulate unknown quantities and solve real problems by resolving the equations. They did little in geometry but preserve Euclid, although they worked out numerous problems using geometry.

The Arabs were excellent astronomers, fine observers. They used all the old information from the Greeks, picked up information from the Chaldean observatories, and then built their own observatories. They corrected Ptolemy's astronomical tables and established their own in several sets. They recognized the precession of the equinoxes (the earlier occurrence of the equinoxes in each successive orbit of the earth around the sun), which Ptolemy did not. They made a solar calendar, studied trigonometry (mathematics concerned with the sides and angles of triangles) and advanced it greatly, creating new tables. Arab sea captains were excellent navigators and apparently adapted the magnetic needle to navigation. They, too, improved on the old astronomical instruments and developed new ones.

Other Arabs advanced the study of mechanics with work in balances and the establishment of specific weights of various substances. They improved the use of pulleys. They built mirrors to work with refraction and reflection, and investigated the properties of light.

The Arabs held that all the natural sciences were applications of the old basic principles of earth, water, fire, and air. They did not divide them into alchemy, zoology, botany, and so forth.

Most Arab alchemists, like others, were misguided by the belief that the magic "elixir of life" existed which could control the elements and even the soul. But practically speaking they contributed much to useful chemical processes. They worked very successfully to determine the specific gravity of various substances. Rhazes classified substances and experimented with them, recording his use of instruments and the steps involved so they might be repeated. The Arabs did not, however, make the basic breakthrough to scientific method, and when they formulated various laws of chemical processes, trying to adjust the known facts to fit the laws, they interjected the nonexistent elixir as a secret ingredient to resolve "insoluble" problems.

The Muslims contributed to the writing of history by putting down the facts about the various dynasties and regimes under which they lived. They corrected errors in Ptolemy's geography and extended the boundaries of the known world, added considerable to the knowledge of agriculture, and introduced a number of fruit plants and others from the East.

Altogether, then, the Arabs and the people they conquered were not simply transmitters of scientific ideas inherited from the Greeks, or even simply combiners who put together ideas from the Greek world and the sciences of India, Persia, and even China. These men were interested in science, they were critical of what they read, heard, and saw, and they attempted to correct errors where they saw them.

In reality, then, there were no Dark Ages for science the way there was for Western society. The center of science simply moved from one culture and linguistic system to another, and then in the twelfth century was ready to move again. What chiefly helped it to move in this period was the general attitude toward learning of the Muslims—the philosophy behind all these achievements. Until the decline of Muslim science and learning, in the wake of the philosophical schisms in the religious community of Islam, the Arabs were relatively uninhibited by religious dogma. Their rulers wanted to learn about the world as it was. Thus, the Muslims were scientific philosophers in their own way. They established a climate for learning and eventually passed along their feeling for knowledge to the West.

To understand why and how science and the other works of the ancients came to Europe, it is necessary to examine a bit more of the complicated social and political history of the Arabs, particularly in the eleventh and twelfth centuries.

In the Near East contact between Baghdad and the western Arabs was cut off by the coming of the Mongols. In the middle Arab kingdom, on the death of Salah al-Din (Saladin) in 1193, the sultanate extended from the Tigris to the Nile, with its capital at Damascus. But within five years that empire began to collapse as various relatives seized portions of it for their own. Salah al-Din's younger brother al-Adil took Egypt and most of Syria. He made peace with the Crusaders and allowed them to establish markets and businesses at Alexandria

and elsewhere. The Franks seized some territory in the
Middle East, lost it, seized more, and the Crusades continued into the middle of the thirteenth century. Then on
the death of Al-Salih Najm al-Din, the last of the rulers
of the family of Salah al-Din, his wife seized power. She
have been a slave, called a *mamluk* in Arabic, and the
dynasty she founded was to be called the Mamluk or
slave dynasty. She married her general, then murdered
him, and was herself murdered in turn. After their
deaths, the man who finally seized power was a Turkoman slave and member of the imperial bodyguard named
Baybars al-Bunduqdari. The Mongols attacked the empire, and he drove them off. He rebuilt the navy, organized the army, and strengthened the forts of Syria,
built a road from Damascus to Cairo and established
a swift postal system using relays of horses. He built
mosques and the Zahiriyah Library in Damascus, which
still stands, and he established a puppet Abbasid caliphate to bring peace and order to the area. He recognized as legitimate all the Shia, Sunni, Sufi, and other
sects into which Islam had split, each with its own qadi
or judge. The Mamluk al-Malik al-Nasir Muhammad
reigned during the last years of the thirteenth and first
years of the fourteenth century, a period that marked the
high point of the culture of Egypt. He cultivated the arts
and learning, built grand mosques and other buildings,
dug a canal that connected Alexandria with the Nile,
and erected public works such as fountains and schools.
There are monuments and fine pieces of pottery and
bronze and jewelry to the Mamluk rule, but the greatness
was gone.

Still, the Syro-Egyptian kingdom led the world these

days in the practice of medical science, in hospital work, and in the treatment of diseases of the eye.

The civilization was ended by Tamerlane (Timur), who swept through Syria in 1400, destroying one city after another, cities that would never be rebuilt. He abandoned his conquest to attend to other matters in the East, but the Syro-Egyptian kingdom was never to recover and not long afterward would fall before the Ottoman Turks.

Obviously, with the exception of the period of rule of al-Malik al-Nasir Muhammad, there was little time in all this history for cultural interchange with the West. Christians and Jews were mistreated and detested, and the climate for transfer of information simply did not exist except for short times in a few places.

But a different climate existed in the third Muslim empire, in Spain. Following the destruction of the Umayyad dynasty, early in the eleventh century, there emerged a series of petty states and petty rulers. During the first half of the century twenty kingdoms held twenty provinces and towns. Then in the north, the petty Christian kingdoms united. Ferdinand I and Alfonso VI united the kingdoms of León, Castile, Galicia, and Navarre, this union brought many Muslims under the rule of Alfonso VII, who was intelligent enough to treat them with respect. To save themselves, the Arabs invited the powerful Berber king, Yusuf ibn-Tashfin, to come and drive away the Christians, and he came in 1086 and defeated the Christians in a bloody battle, soon took possession of Granada and Seville, and then won nearly all of Muslim Spain. Toledo remained in the hands of Alfonso VII, but it was still a Muslim city. The language

was Arabic and even the coins were stamped with
Arabic characters.

The Berbers ruled almost unmolested until the thirteenth century. Then, in 1212, a combined army of
Christians from Aragon, Navarre, and Portugal, met a
large Muslim force on a hill seventy miles east of Cordova and defeated the Muslims as decisively as Yusuf
had won the day a century and a quarter earlier. The
country was split up among Christian and Muslim rulers,
Granada becoming the capital of Muhammad ibn-Yusuf
ibn-Nasr, also known as ibn-al-Ahmar. There, among
Christians and Jews, al-Ahmar built the Alhambra, and
for a brief moment in history Granada rivaled old Cordova as a center of culture and learning. Granada became the wealthiest city in Spain, and travelers flocked
there. By the middle of the thirteenth century, nearly all
of the rest of Spain was in Christian hands. One might
say, then, that in the twelfth and thirteenth centuries,
the cultural island of Granada stood out for the Christians to see, and they were impressed with its bright
beacon.

The christianization of Spain was a gradual process.
When the Spanish kings conquered various cities and
provinces, they met an Arabic-speaking population. So
common was this situation in the twelfth and thirteenth
centuries that there was a word for Arabic-speaking
Muslims who lived under Christian domination. They
were called *mudejars*. They were not mistreated, but as
time went on, they began to speak the Romance language
of their conquerors and began to forget their Arabic. In
the fifteenth century the kingdoms of Aragon and Castile were united in the marriage of Ferdinand and Isa-

bella, and swiftly then the Christians moved to conquer
all of Spain, and on January 2, 1492, Ferdinand and
Isabella's forces entered Granada and Muslim rule was
ended.

Ferdinand and Isabella set out to destroy the Muslim
civilization. Arabic manuscripts were burned in the
squares of Granada. As time went on the Muslims were
persecuted and finally driven from Spain altogether, but
in the period when the Christians were not yet strong
enough to conquer Spain and yet could overrun certain
parts of it, there was much mingling of the cultures of
Christian Europe and the Muslim world, and it is this
period, particularly in the twelfth century, when the
results of Islamic science were passed on to the West.

From the seventh century, while the star of Islam was
rising, the brightness that had been Rome was decayed
and dying. This period was marked in the West by political confusion, military uprising, and looting on the
part of barbarian tribes of Europe, economic recession
in the stifling of Europe's trade with the East, and the
clinging to the Roman Church as the one stable element
in a disintegrated society. These were known as the Dark
Ages of Europe. The darkness began to fall in the fifth
century.

Mysticism and magic also helped destroy the founda-
tions of science in the Roman Empire, and when the empire was split up with the overthrow of the last of the
Western emperors by Odoacer in the fifth century, even
the Latin language degenerated.

A handful of scholars remained. Rome's Boethius
put down the knowledge of Aristotle, and wrote in the
sixth century on logic, arithmetic, music, geometry, and

astronomy. But a handful does not make a civilization, and although Boethius' pupil Cassiodorus prepared a bibliography that was also an introduction to science, and Isidore, the bishop of Seville, wrote an encyclopedia of European knowledge, there were few others. The Venerable Bede in the eighth century did some study of arithmetic. In the ninth century the Irish astronomer Dicuil wrote a geography that did have new descriptions of Egypt and the Northern Islands. Johannes Scotus Erigena adapted an old Greek cosmology which held that the sun, the moon, and the superior planets revolved around the earth, while Venus and Mercury revolve around the sun and that a day is marked by the rotation of the earth around its own axis. Erigena extended this idea to include the rotation of Mars and Jupiter around the sun. That was a cosmology, an old-fashioned one and not satisfactory even to explain the apparent movements in the heavens, but it was the best that was being done in Europe, at a time when the Muslims were beginning the intensive and critical study of Ptolemaic astronomy.

Between the Battle of Tours in 732 and the end of the tenth century, European science simply stood still, even as it boiled and bubbled in the world of Islam.

Gerbert, the monk who became Sylvester II, represents the first link between Muslim Spain and Christian Europe. He lived in the Christian community of Vichy toward the end of the tenth century, and he studied at the Catalan monastery of Santa Maria de Ripoll, where Arabic ideas had infiltrated from the south. He wrote a friend in Barcelona asking for a treatise on astrology, which contained information on the use of the astrolabe.

It was he who first brought this instrument to Europe. He also wrote the bishop of Gerona for a work on multiplication and division. At about the time of Gerbert, the Arabic-Hindu numerals came to the West, although their use was restricted to a very small group of students.

When a school was established at Salerno in Sicily, at first it was independent of Muslim influence, but then, with Constantinus Africanus and others, the ideas of Islam began to find their way into the educational pattern.

In the tenth century the monks at Santa Maria de Ripoll were translating from Arabic to Latin works dealing with the construction and use of the astrolabe. They were also translating documents dealing with geometry and giving descriptions of such instruments as the gnomon.

By the eleventh century, a Christian monk named Hermann Contractus was aware of the impact of Arabic science, even though he worked in the Richenau monastery on an island in Lake Constance, far indeed from Spain. He wrote about astrolabes, and his information must have come from some Arabic sources.

The most important translator of the twelfth century was Pedro Alfonso, a Spanish Jew who became a convert to Christianity. He was known primarily as a theological writer, but he translated several works dealing with astronomy and medicine from Arabic to Latin.

He was physician to Alfonso VI, the king of Castile, and then he visited England, where for a time he served as physician to King Henry I. In England Pedro Alfonso made several converts to science, including Walcher, the prior of Malvern. Walcher had lived in Italy and knew something of the achievements of the Arabic-speaking world in astronomy. He wanted to secure the best instruments from the Muslims, especially for observing eclipses. Walcher wrote a book on astronomy which was based on an original work by Pedro Alfonso. This book discussed the waxing and waning of the moon, the methods of determining the position of the sun, and the way of calculating eclipses. Later Pedro Alfonso wrote an introduction to one of his works directed to the philosophical students of France. This is another way Arab science came to the West. In the eleventh century it was beginning to spread far and fast.

The next important contributor was Adelard of Bath, an acquaintance of Pedro Alfonso. Adelard was a philosopher and a student. After years of travel in the Arab world, he wrote a dialogue called *Questiones Naturales,* in which seventy-six chapters treat with scientific questions and try to answer each with the knowledge of the Arabs.

Adelard also explained the principles of arithmetic, astronomy, geometry, and music, as he had learned them from reading Arabic works. At the time, however, he had apparently not read the work of Euclid, for geometry was very scantily handled. Later he did study Euclid and translated the fifteen books from the Arabic into Latin.

Studying in Tarsus and Antioch, he became thoroughly familiar with the astrolabe and other Arabic astronomical instruments, translated a treatise on astrology by the Arabic writer abu Maashar Jaafar, and wrote a paper on the preparation of pigments.

In the second quarter of the twelfth century, Adelard

had completed his studies of Arabic and was back in England, bent on making the knowledge of the Muslims available to the people of his own land. To do so, he translated works on subjects that ranged from trigonometry to falconry, philosophy, and astrology.

He was the first northern European to assimilate Arab science, and he was the man who brought Euclid to the West. He also brought the beginnings of the new astronomy.

The next notable European students were a pair: John of Seville and Domingo Gundislavo. They lived and worked in Toledo under the patronage of Raymond I, the archbishop of Toledo between 1125 and 1150. John translated from Arabic into Castilian and Domingo put the Castilian into Latin. These translations included works on astronomy, astrology, philosophy, arithmetic, and medicine. They brought knowledge of zero and square roots to the West. Much deep and important knowledge came quickly to Europe, thanks to such devoted translators as this pair.

In astronomy and astrology they translated the works of Mashallah, of the eighth century, who assisted with the survey for the foundation of Baghdad. They translated al-Farghani's *Elements of Astronomy,* from the ninth century, a book which dealt with celestial motions and the complete science of the stars as known to the Greeks, using Ptolemy's theory of the precession of the equinoxes and giving figures for the distances and dimensions of the planets. This work became basic to European astronomy until the fifteenth century. The pair translated Abu Mashar's *Great Book of the Introduction,* another astronomical and astrological work that contained a theory of the tides and this was widely accepted in Europe. Next came the work of al-Kindi, also of the ninth century at Baghdad. Again the interest was in astrological work. That was the basic point of interest in Europe at the time.

Umar ibn-al-Farrukhan also wrote on the principles of astrology. Al-Battani was one of the great Islamic astronomers, but Europeans translated his astrological work rather than his great astronomical treatise. They did do some work on astronomy, too, including rewriting in Latin the books of Thabit ibn-Qurrems, the astronomer, to add to the eight Ptolemaic spheres a ninth one *(primum mobile)* to account for what he believed to be the trepidation of the equinoxes. His theory was wrong, but his mathematics and his observational powers were excellent. So Europe was the wiser for it.

From the second half of the tenth century, John and Domingo chose al-Qabisi's *Introduction to the Art of Astrology* and his book on judicial astrology, but they also translated this student's work on the conjunction of planets, which was not astrological. From the same period they chose Maslama ibn-Ahmad, the Cordovan astronomer, and translated his work on the astrolabe.

In the field of medicine, they translated the famous pseudo-Aristotelian work *Secretum Secretorum,* a compilation of fact, folklore, and superstition regarding physical makeup and diet. It seems an odd choice, but it represented a popular interest, one that continued to be popular in nearly every European country.

In philosophy the scholars translated the Neoplatonic *Liber de Causis,* which was an abstract of the work of the Alexandrian philosopher and encyclopedist Proclus,

and then they wrote a commentary on his work. Proclus
had written extensively on Hesiod, Plato, Aristotle,
Euclid, and Ptolemy. He had studied astronomy and
mathematics as well as philosophy, and his writings indicated the breadth and depth of his knowledge. From
the first half of the ninth century the translators chose
the important philosopher al-Kindi and translated one
of his works, *De Intellectu.*

They also translated the work of a Christian philosopher, doctor, and astronomer who lived in Syria, the
great al-Farabi. His *Fundamentals of Science* was basic
material for the West. From ibn-Sina (Avicenna)
Europeans took a philosophical dialogue. Ibn-Gabirol
(Avicebrón) became very famous in the West through
this translation, and was sometimes called the Jewish
Plato. John and Domingo also took al-Ghazzali's *Maqa-
sid al-Falasifa,* an encyclopedia which dealt with logic,
physics, and metaphysics.

Their work was continued by Hermann the Carinthian.
A student in France in the first years of the twelfth century, he then moved to Spain for seven years. Later
Hermann transferred to Languedoc in southern France
and then for some time was connected with the cathedral
school at Chartres. He is best known for the valuable
service he gave in translating Ptolemy's *Planisphere* into
Latin from the Arabic. The reason he used the Arabic is
that the original Greek work of the *Planisphere* was
lost, so the West would not have the information today
had it not been for Hermann's translation of Massama's
version.

Hermann's life is an indication of the growth of in-
tellectuality in the West. He was a Slav by birth, but he

journeyed to France. There he came under the influence of Thierry of Chartres, one of the great teachers of the period. Thierry had been quick to scent the "new" ideas of Aristotle, and encouraged the young Slav to go to Spain, learn the language, and begin reaping the fruits of Arab scholarship. By the autumn of 1138 Hermann knew enough Arabic to make his first translation. Next came translations of al-Khwarizmi and Albumasar. Finally he was sufficiently informed to write a treatise of his own, *De Essentiis,* a philosophical study of "five essences" he believed to have permanent existence. It is valuable for miscellaneous information on astronomy and geography.

In about 1142 Hermann was in León, and then he went into Toulouse, and later to Béziers. He became a good friend with Robert of Chester, another translator, and they often worked together.

De Essentiis indicates a basic change in the thinking of Western scholars. Hermann's early education came from sources that had not been exposed to the learning of Islam. But by the time of his writing this book he had become familiar with the Greek and Roman greats: Seneca, Macrobius, Vitruvius, Hesiod, and much of Aristotle. He knew Euclid and Ptolemy, and Eratosthenes, Hipparchus, and Archimedes. All this familiarity with the past came from Arabic works.

Robert of Chester, working alongside Hermann part of the time, translated al-Kindi's *Judicia* and made the first translation of the Koran, so that Westerners might understand the philosophy of Islam more completely. Robert was interested in alchemy. He also translated the algebra of al-Khwarizmi, and thus brought to the Western world that part of mathematics for the first time. He translated a small Ptolemy treatise on the astrolabe and, using his new astronomy, prepared astronomical tables for the longitude of London, based on the tables of al-Battani in the second half of the ninth century and those of al-Zarqali in the second half of the eleventh century. So it can be seen that these translators were carriers as well, using their knowledge to make the material most useful to the West.

Of all the translators who helped bring the fruits of Muslim civilization to Europe, probably the most important was Gerard of Cremona, an Italian scholar who was born about 1114 in Cremona, Lombardy.

In the course of his education, Gerard learned of the existence of the *Almagest,* that huge work by Ptolemy, which represented the culmination of Greek astronomical thought. The *Almagest* had been translated into Arabic in the ninth century and was so highly regarded by the Muslims that much investigative and critical writing had been based on the work. So it was no surprise that, even though he had not seen the *Almagest* and could not read Arabic, Gerard should learn of its existence and become interested in studying it. Gerard went to Toledo, then, to see the *Almagest.* He remained to learn Arabic and spend the remainder of his life translating the scholastic works of the Muslim community.

In the course of that life, Gerard translated and wrote nearly ninety books including the *Almagest.* Some of these translated works were so long that it seemed impossible one man could do so much. Ibn-Sina's *Xanun fi-l-Tibb,* for example, comprised a million words.

Gerard did so many translations that modern scholars

finally came to the conclusion that Gerard represented the whole School of Toledo, and that many of the works that were issued under his name were either not done by him or were done under his general supervision.

His translations of the *Almagest* was completed in Toledo in 1175. A better translation had been done fifteen years earlier in Sicily. But the Sicilian translation sat in a musty vault and was scarcely known, while Gerard's became the standard work, bringing the wisdom of Ptolemy to Europe.

15

The Assimilation of Arab Science

ONE OF the early indications of the effect of Arabic science on the West was given by Walcher, the prior of Malvern, a friend of Pedro Alfonso, the Spanish scholar who spent some time in England. In 1091, while traveling in Italy, Walcher observed an eclipse. The next year Walcher observed the eclipse of October 18, and he used an astrolabe so the new knowledge was having practical effects.

At about that same time another scholar, Roger of Hereford, wrote a book comparing the astronomy of the Latins with that of the Hebrews and Chaldeans—which shows a considerable body of knowledge.

Translations and knowledge began coming up from Syria, too. The man called Stephen of Antioch was a native of Pisa who studied first at the schools of Sicily and then went to Antioch, where he spent his life translating medical writings. The merchants of Amalfi had an active trade with Constantinople and Syria, and this was a channel for some scientific information. Still most of the information passed to Europe in this period came from the Arabic-speaking lands, and in this, besides Spain and Syria, Sicily played a large role because the kingdom there was Norman, by conquest. In the two Sicilies, Greek, Arabic, and Latin were in constant use.

The Normans of Palermo had close contact with the homeland in the north, and the monks at St. Michel, Bec, and other centers of learning were aware of what was going on in the south. Many English and French monks came to Palermo, Syracuse, and other cities to study and then took their new learning back with them.

Frederick II of Sicily encouraged his scholars to independent thought, although his methods were not all they might be. It is said he once shut a man up in a barrel to discover if he could see the man's soul depart when he died, and he once had two men disemboweled to examine the effects on the alimentary canal. But his interest in science, if bloody, was real. He kept a running correspondence with various other kings on mathematical, astronomical, and philosophical problems.

The relations between Frederick's court and the Muslims were stronger than those of the previous Sicilian kings. Michael Scot, one of Frederick's principal scientific advisers, came to Sicily as an expert on Spanish-Arab learning. He translated a number of Arabic works. He knew Arabian astronomy. Frederick also kept another scientist named Theodore, whose major duty was to carry on Frederick's correspondence in Arabic with kings and sultans of the east.

Frederick was very much predisposed toward the learning of Islam, and he kept strengthening his relations with the rulers of Muslim states. In 1232 al-Ashraf, the sultan of Damascus, sent Frederick a present he admired very much: a planetarium with figures of the sun and moon marking the hours. In this letter, Frederick asked the sultan questions of mathematics and philosophy, which the sultan answered in his own handwriting.

Frederick had a habit of posing difficult questions in his letters to the Muslim rulers. In 1240 he sent a series of questions to al-Rashid, the caliph of Morocco. The caliph forwarded the questions to a Spanish Arab philosopher, ibn-Sabin, who was living in Ceuta. The philosopher answered them.

Frederick also asked a series of geometrical questions of the mathematician Jehuda ben Solomon Cohen in Toledo. He sent other questions to the sultan of Egypt, al-Malik al-Kamil. For example: Why do objects partly covered by water appear bent? Why does Canopus appear larger when near the horizon, when in the southern deserts the absence of moisture precludes moisture as an explanation? What is the cause of the illusion of spots before the eyes?

Thus Frederick's court was the most intellectual of Europe. Meanwhile Alfonso X of Castile began absorbing more knowledge from the Arab world. Alfonso was a learned man, a student of astronomy and history. He dreamed of publishing an encyclopedia of all human knowledge, and during his reign one important segment was finished. It was *Libros del Saber de Astronomia,* which leaned heavily on the astronomical knowledge of Muslim Spain. Included were a description of the known stars and the celestial sphere, and accounts of the major instruments of astronomy, the astrolabe, the quadrant, and various clocks. Another important work, hardly a book for it was nearly all figures, was the Alphonsine Tables, which remained the most important astronomical tables of Europe until the sixteenth century.

The case of the Alphonsine Tables is an illustration, of a principal reason for the rapid spread of both the old Arabic science and Latin science of this period. The

Alphonsine Tables were written in Spanish, not in Latin. They were up-to-date and valuable to any astronomer in the West, but because they were composed in a language understood by relatively few people, they did not reach the scientific centers such as Paris for nearly half a century. Other materials, such as the translations of Ptolemy's *Almagest,* spread immediately throughout the centers of civilization because they were written in Latin.

The schools of translation into Latin, then, had a *basic* impact on the spread of scientific knowledge in the West. In the eleventh and twelfth centuries these schools were assisted by schools of another kind, the cathedral schools of the church, such as that at Chartres. Next, were to come the universities.

There had been universities of a sort in the world before the thirteenth century. In the fourth century Plato had founded the Academy at Athens, which persisted until A.D. 529. The Academy was a center of higher education in philosophy, mathematics, music, and astronomy. In about 335 B.C. Plato's disciple Aristotle founded the Lyceum, with its Peripatetic School of philosophy. Here he carried on enormous researches in botany, zoology, anatomy, and did his encyclopedic writing, which included learned discussions of nearly every subject known to the Greeks.

Later the Museum of Alexandria was founded. After the Greeks, came the House of Learning of Baghdad, which was also a university of sorts, the Dar al-Hikma of Cairo, and the great mosque university of Cordova. There were similar advanced schools in Palestine, China, and India.

But by the twelfth century a new concept came to a

reviving Europe, the idea of an organization of teachers and pupils, established in one place, carrying on a definite course of studies. By 1208 the idea of the university was approved by Pope Innocent III. Salerno was one more or less confined to medicines. Bologna, in the twelfth century, was a famous law school.

The University of Paris drew from three church schools in that city, principally from the school of the Cathedral of Notre Dame. The earliest college of the university was established about 1180 by an Englishman named Josce of London. It was not long before there were students and faculties of four schools, arts, law, medicine, and theology.

At Montpellier, Peter of Piacenza established a school of law. Then a medical school was established, teaching in Hebrew and Arabic. But this teaching was soon replaced by instruction in Latin and by the twelfth century Latin was the language of the school.

Oxford was established in the middle of the twelfth century; Cambridge became an educational center just after the beginning of the thirteenth century.

By the thirteenth century enough of Aristotle had been translated from the Arabic, thanks to Gerard of Cremona and others, that the study was introduced into the University of Paris. With this development, Muslim science was almost completely absorbed in the West. Encyclopedists, such as Vincent of Beauvais, were summarizing the scientific knowledge of the day. Other men made individual contributions. Albertus Magnus became a great naturalist, studying plant physiology and carrying on such investigations as a dissection of the eye of a mole and a study of the nervous system of the crayfish.

Others conducted experiments in optics, magnetism, and other scientific subjects. Herman the Lame improved the astrolabe. Others improved it more. Still others invented new instruments for astronomical observation.

The West, in other words, had seized the torch of science and learning from a failing East, just as the Arabs had taken it from the dying Graeco-Roman society. The process was described by Bernard of Chartres: "We are like dwarfs placed upon the shoulders of giants who can see better and further than giants, not because our vision is more acute and our stature greater, but because we have raised ourselves above them."

So, science was like a building, each society laying a course of bricks. It began with the Babylonians and the ancients of the Indus Valley. The later inhabitants of the Fertile Crescent contributed. So did the Greeks and the Persians and the Hindus and even the Chinese, although to a major extent the Chinese tradition remained in the East. All these people had laid the bricks for the Arabs, and after they established Muslim society, how good a job they did too!

Bibliography

Bodenheim, Friedrich Simon, *The History of Biology*. London: W. Dawson, 1958.

Browne, Edward, *Arabian Medicine*. Cambridge, England: Cambridge University Press, 1921.

Castiglioni, Arturo, *History of Medicine*. New York: Alfred Knopf, 1947.

Delambré, Jean Baptiste Joseph, *L'Historie de l'Astronomie du Moyen Age*. Paris: Courcier, 1819.

Glubb, John Bagot, *The Great Arab Conquests*. London: Hodder and Stoughton, 1963.

Hitti, Philip K., *History of the Arabs*. London: Macmillan, 1967.

Izzeddin, Nejla, *The Arab World*. London, n.d.

Mieli, Aldo, *La Science Arabe*. Leiden, E. J. Brill, 1938.

Muller, Herbert J., *The Loom of History*. New York: Oxford University Press, 1966.

Multauf, Robert P., *The Origins of Chemistry*. London: Oldbourne, 1966.

Musil, Alois, *The Manners and Customs of the Ruwala Bedouins*. New York: Czech Academy of Sciences and Arts, and Charles R. Crane, 1928.

——— *In the Arabian Desert*, New York: H. Liveright, 1930.

Nasr, Seyyed Hossein, *Science and Civilization in Islam*.

Nutting, Anthony, *The Arabs*. New York: C. N. Potter, 1966.

Palter, Robert, *Toward Modern Science*. New York: Farrar, Straus and Company, 1961.

Sarton, George, *Introduction to the History of Science*. Baltimore: Williams and Wilkins, 1927.

Sayili, Aydin, *The Observatory in Islam*. Ankara, Turkey: Tarih Kurumu Basimevy, 1960.

Taton, Rene, *History of Science*. New York: Basic Books. 1964–65.

Index